PRA
LIVE FC

"Careers today are less predictable than ever. In this wonderful book, Paula Caligiuri and Andy Palmer show that this should be a source of excitement, not dread. *Live for a Living* will help you identify your talents, develop your goals, and turn your unpredictable career into an adventure."

—ARTHUR C. BROOKS, PHD, professor, Harvard Kennedy School and Harvard Business School; #1 *New York Times* best-selling author

"Bold, enlightening, and packed with wisdom, *Live for a Living* offers an inspiring message that will resonate with anyone seeking to unlock their true potential. Take the reins of your career and let your talents shine!"

—CHRISTOPHER AHLBERG, PHD, CEO and co-founder, Recorded Future

"*Live for a Living* provides the tools and insights needed to craft the career that works for you. Filled with practical advice, this book inspires readers to align their careers with their passions, creating a life filled with purpose and joy. A compelling read for anyone looking to redefine success on their own terms."

—ELISE AWWAD, president and CEO, DeVry University

"In today's fast-paced world, 'time is the coin of the realm,' and we seldom have the time to reflect on the why and how of our journey (i.e., where we are headed). *Live for a Living* offers a way to embrace our full selves—the quality and quantity of our personal and professional time—to clarify our purpose, and to achieve significance and meaning in our career and work-life integration."

—DANA H. BORN, PHD, brigadier general (USAFA retired); lecturer, Harvard Kennedy School

"Most people don't marry the first person they meet on a dating app or at a salsa class. Likewise, finding a fulfilling career requires a great deal of effort, experimentation, and a plan. This book provides a compelling guide for doing just that. A must-read for anyone at a career crossroads."

—TOMAS CHAMORRO-PREMUZIC, PHD, chief innovation officer, ManpowerGroup; author of *I, Human: AI, Automation, and the Quest to Reclaim What Makes Us Unique*

"With a powerful blend of practical advice and soul-searching exercises, *Live for a Living* will empower you to dig deep and uncover your unique gifts. It's more than a career guide; it's a life manual for those ready to take control of their destiny."

—RICH MINER, PHD, co-founder, Android, Inc.

"*Live for a Living* is a clear guidebook for those seeking a more fulfilling, authentic, and self-directed relationship with their careers. Paula and Andy systematically navigate you to discover a renewed sense of purpose and agency so you can savor each tender stage of your career journey. An important read!"

—ANNE JACOBY, CEO, Spring Street Solutions; author of *Born to Create: How Creativity Sparks Connection, Innovation, and Belonging in our New World of Work*

"A game-changer for anyone feeling stuck in their career. *Live for a Living* is an insightful book that provides the keys to understanding your purpose and guides you to a fulfilling career aligned with your passions and strengths. Don't miss out on this transformative read!"

—FRANK MOSS, PHD, entrepreneur; former director, MIT Media Lab

"In *Live for a Living*, the authors brilliantly encapsulate the essence of the changing career landscape amid the global challenges faced in the wake of the pandemic. They seamlessly interweave poignant reflections from the past, stark realities of the present, and hopeful visions for the future, all geared toward empowering individuals to take charge of their career destinies. This work serves as a timely beacon for those seeking purpose, balance, and fulfillment in their professional and personal lives."

—AMY ELIZA WONG, author of the critically acclaimed *Living On Purpose: Five Deliberate Choices to Realize Fulfillment and Joy*

PAULA CALIGIURI, PhD
& ANDY PALMER

WORK LIVE

FOR A

LIVING

HOW *to* CREATE *Your* CAREER JOURNEY

to WORK HAPPIER, NOT HARDER

FAST
COMPANY
Press

Fast Company Press
New York, New York
www.fastcompanypress.com

This work is being published under the Fast Company Press imprint by an
exclusive arrangement with *Fast Company*. *Fast Company* and the *Fast Company*
logo are registered trademarks of Mansueto Ventures, LLC. The Fast Company
Press logo is a wholly owned trademark of Mansueto Ventures, LLC.

Distributed by River Grove Books

Design and composition by Greenleaf Book Group and Brian Phillips
Cover design by Greenleaf Book Group and Brian Phillips
Author photograph by Jack McGoldrick

Publisher's Cataloging-in-Publication data is available.

Print ISBN: 978-1-63908-085-4

eBook ISBN: 978-1-63908-086-1

First Edition

To my late parents, with enduring gratitude for their wisdom and love.
Their example shaped my career and touched these pages.

—PAULA

To my kids, Morgan, Jonah, Annie, Gerry, and Heather, and my
granddaughters, Raelynn and Skylar, with hopes for great work lives.

—ANDY

PAULA CALIGIURI, PhD
& ANDY PALMER

CONTENTS

INTRODUCTION

When Paula wrote *Get a Life, Not a Job*, it was in response to the economic downturn of the Great Recession from 2007 to 2009. During that time, a heavy emotional toll was paid by those who were too nervous to leave their unfulfilling jobs during a period of high unemployment. The magnitude of layoffs during the Great Recession was staggering, as many hardworking and loyal employees were terminated without regard to their years of dedication or stellar performance reviews. During that time, people globally learned a valuable collective lesson: **to take greater ownership of one's career and not rely on an employer.**

During that Great Recession time, many people became less focused on moving up a corporate ladder and more focused on being marketable for the next opportunity. There was less lifetime employment. Employees started to own their careers. They continually prepared themselves for their next job by creating strong personal brands and engaging professional networks. Since the Great Recession, there have been fifteen years of experience in "owning one's career" which should have resulted in a high level of collective career satisfaction. Unfortunately, job satisfaction remains low. There has been career ownership, but without the skills needed to self-develop a great career. *Live for a Living* helps you build those skills.

We believe the time is right in today's zeitgeist for people to use their personal career journey to find deep career fulfillment. There are a few factors propelling this need. Around the world, starting in early 2020, the COVID-19 pandemic forced lockdowns and quarantines. The death toll was tragic, and the anxiety was palpable. Many who were working at the start of the pandemic were unemployed, furloughed, or worked in makeshift home offices at the kitchen table alongside their children who were restlessly attending school remotely. The lockdowns forced us to change our daily routines, try new things, cook more, use technology to interact, and reframe the basics of what was important in our lives. Identifying what was important took on a new meaning.

Except for frontline workers and health providers, those who experienced intense loneliness, or those who had healthcare concerns for themselves or loved ones, the pandemic had a thin silver lining: more time to think and rebalance life's priorities. Many people globally did exactly that. When they stopped to consider what was important in their lives, many found that they were happy with several aspects of their personal lives. *But their work lives?* Not so much. The result: employees started quitting their jobs at an unprecedented and alarming rate.

This period (which started in 2021) has been referred to as the *Great Resignation*, the *Great Reset*, and the *Great Reimagination*.[1] Whatever it was called, for many workers it felt *great*. The "Great Resignation" refers to a trend of workers leaving their jobs in large numbers during the COVID-19 pandemic.[2] While there is no one cause for this phenomenon, there are several factors believed to have contributed to the trend, including the following:

- **Pandemic-related burnout and stress:** Many workers have been working from home, dealing with long hours, increased workloads, and isolation from colleagues, all while trying to manage personal and family responsibilities during the pandemic. This has led to increased burnout and stress levels, prompting some workers to reassess the role their job had in their well-being, and quit jobs that were unfulfilling or stressful.

- **The availability of remote work**: The pandemic has accelerated the trend of remote work, with many companies allowing their employees to work from home permanently or at least part-time. For some, being able to access the office without having to wear work clothes or commute was a wonderful opportunity for increased productivity. This has given workers more flexibility and autonomy, and some have decided to leave their jobs to pursue opportunities that offer more remote work options.

- **The search for better work/life balance**: The pandemic has caused many workers to reassess their work/life balance and prioritize their personal lives over their careers. Some have decided to leave their jobs to pursue careers that offer more flexibility and a better work/ life balance.

- **Generational shifts**: As the workforce continues to become more diverse, there has been a generational shift in attitudes toward work. Younger workers tend to prioritize job satisfaction and purpose over job security and stability and are more likely to switch jobs if they feel their current job is not fulfilling.

- **Increased job opportunities**: Despite the pandemic, some industries have experienced growth and are hiring. This has created more job opportunities and given workers more options to find a job that better suits their needs and interests.

These are just some of the influences that configure differently depending on country, location, industry, and job type. Whether the situation is palpable in your country and industry, we'd like you to think of this moment in time in a different way—as a **Great Opportunity**. Today's climate is one in which you can feel empowered with a heightened sense of autonomy and control, have greater clarity of your priorities, and align your career around the life you want to live. You can design your career to *Live for a Living*.

What does the *Great Opportunity* mean for you?

We wrote this book because we know that old habits die hard. While career fulfillment is possible for many, it is too easy to return to a well-worn path of your former career habits. We wrote this book because we want you to have the skills needed to seize the Great Opportunity and start a new career journey, one that will give you greater career fulfillment.

Live for a Living is a guide to designing your life that includes your career—expanding and directing your career purposefully to do more of what you enjoy and move closer to your ideal. We offer an approach that has more professional excitement, personal fulfillment, and financial security.

More than anything, we hope the tools and tips in this book inspire you to remain in control of your career and your life. We want you to build self-awareness to identify an ideal career goal and, in turn, craft the *career acts* to reach your goal.

Paula originally introduced "career acts" in *Get a Life, Not a Job* over a decade ago. It was a way to think about what you do for income and experience in more manageable, less permanent pieces. Career acts are like mosaic pieces. Each piece is stimulating skill-enhancing and income-generating activity that are both engaging and growth-oriented. They combine together so you can progress toward your ideal career, whether an occupation, a purpose, or both. Career acts can be accomplished while working for an employer or for yourself. Working for yourself is easier than ever before in a world more open to the gig economy where digital solutions have democratized entry into business ventures, and where we can test, revise, and develop new opportunities at a far faster rate. We also appreciate that being self-employed is not the right path for many. We provide many ways to craft the career that works for you.

In this book, we will encourage you to limit your preoccupation with head-hunters and what you think your next employer might want to see on your résumé. These are becoming less important compared to the self-development of skills and self-directed career moves. Instead of the old career path directed solely by an employer, we encourage you to try a new one that places your

4

interests, needs, talents, and motivators as the signposts for the career choices you make. Simply put, we propose that the best career journey is continual self-directed and goal-oriented self-development. The best career journey is not beholden to any company-run training platform or career paths that head-hunters chose for you.

In no part of this book do we promise any type of career nirvana. Regardless of how much you love what you do for a living, you'll still need to engage with "work." Work, at times, will be frustrating, exhausting, confusing, and ambiguous. While we cannot provide career nirvana, we can provide guidance to find the career acts that are fun and fulfilling for you.

We do our best to make the case that perpetually chasing *shiny new jobs* without a more thoughtful plan sets you up for continued career frustration. This is the path to nowhere. At the same time, we do not advocate stepping away from a great job into a fantasy land where you take reckless risks on a dream entrepreneurial venture, nor do we fill you with unrealistic expectations that a vaulted corporate position or entrepreneurial success can happen overnight. That would be snake oil. Great careers and the career acts along the way require effort.

In chapter 1, we give you the tools to diagnose your career readiness, focusing on your current relationship with your career. In chapter 2, we provide a way to build self-awareness needed to help you uncover your natural strengths, motivators, and how you like to work. Chapter 3 uses that knowledge to help you identify your ideal career goal. Chapter 4 helps you craft the career acts you will need along your journey to achieve that goal. In chapter 5, we encourage you, if interested, to consider sources of income like an investment portfolio and create multiple simultaneous career acts. Recognizing that many people prefer one source of income through an employer, chapter 6 provides tips for creating a safety net with your employer and advice on career success within an organization. Whether you use a diversified or single employer approach, chapter 7 offers tips for how to balance your career with your other life priorities.

The last part of the book (chapters 8 and 9) describes how to gain more of the resources you need for a fulfilling career. Focusing on your whole life, and not just your career, chapter 8 delves into specific strategies to increase your physical and emotional well-being. Chapter 9 identifies a great source of stress for many—the need for greater amounts of time and money—and offers suggestions for better utilization and preservation of both.

Online assessments to tailor the book

To make this book more tailored to your situation, we encourage you to work through the assessments found on www.myJournii.com. These self-assessments will help you apply the suggestions in this book to your own career in real time. If you take the self-assessments as you read the book, our advice will speak more directly to your situation.

Diagnose your relationship with your career

A good place to start your Live for a Living journey is to diagnose the state of your relationship with your career. To what extent are you able to answer "yes" to the following:

1. Your career is directed by you such that you know what your next career act needs to be.

2. Your career is based on your talents, interests, and motivators.

3. Your career is well integrated into your life, providing you with the level of work/life harmony you seek.

4. You have a sense of freedom because, while you work hard, you do not feel beholden to either the employer for which you work or the business you run.

5. You feel empowered to achieve the income you seek.

6. You are inspired and energized by the work you do.

7. You spend time during each workday in a state of flow, doing something you love.

How many of these statements apply to you in your current situation? If the answer is "all of the above" then you might want to pass this book along to a friend who is not so fortunate. If you only answered "yes" to a few of these statements, please join us for the rest of this book. As you put some of these suggestions into practice, we'd love to hear how your answers to these questions change over time.

A bit about us

Throughout the book you will hear more about our careers and the career acts that got us to where we are today. As friends with little professional overlap, our collaboration on this book seems an unlikely one on the surface. Andy built his career in technology and life sciences and is currently the CEO of Tamr and the founder of the private equity firm Koa Labs, with about one hundred companies in his portfolio at various stages. He has taken wild risks, has a broad diversity of roles, and has enjoyed the associated high rewards. Paula built her career as an academic with deep roots in the field of organizational psychology, with expertise on how to develop individuals' cultural agility. As the co-founder (with Andy) of the public benefit corporation Skiilify, her professional purpose is to place professional skill development into the hands, hearts, and minds of anyone who wants them.

We believe that our differences will demonstrate to you some diversity in how a career journey can unfold. At the same time, our similarities help you understand our shared philosophy for work. We are both self-made, working hard for what we have achieved. We both believe in education, experience, and effort. We both have made mistakes in both our careers and our personal lives. These mistakes have made us wiser, more resilient, and better able to prioritize. We both follow the advice we offer (and wish we had done so earlier in our careers). We both gain deep satisfaction from mentoring, especially when we can help mentees see possibilities they could not have otherwise seen. We both see this current moment as a great opportunity for you to have more personal control and fulfillment from work.

In these pages, we offer cases of many people who have outstanding careers. They run the gamut on almost every dimension: age, education, family situation, and so on. They share a love for what they do for a living. As you will read, their lives are enviable and inspirational—but also highly motivating in their honesty. They provide the evidence that all of us can attain fulfilling careers and lives. We are inspired by them and hope you are too.

Happy reading,
Paula and Andy

PART 1

IDENTIFY YOUR CAREER GOAL

CHAPTER 1

HAVE A BETTER RELATIONSHIP WITH YOUR CAREER

The biggest adventure you can ever take is to live the life of your dreams.
—OPRAH WINFREY

"You don't have to work for a big company or an established company to make a living. You can create your own company. There's another way to work," says Alberto Bravo, describing his ideal career.[1]

He should know. What started out as a chance on-the-job meeting with a coworker at a giant accounting firm eventually spawned a thirty-five-person virtual company called *We Are Knitters*. With earnings of 15–16 million euros in 2021, the company today boasts a worldwide virtual community of more than six hundred thousand passionate knitters.

Armed with business degrees from good universities, Alberto and Pepita Marin had landed prestigious jobs at the international accounting power-house PwC in Madrid in 2008. Meeting at a master-level university class held by PwC for junior associates, they became fast friends. The two found they shared a love of fashion along with a strong belief that PwC just wasn't for them. They dreamed about someday starting a business in fashion, although admittedly lacked the skills required to put their shared passion to work. They would need design skills or retailing experience to differentiate their company from others like Zara or H&M.

On holiday to visit friends in New York City, they observed something unexpected. They saw trendy and well-dressed women in their twenties **knitting** on the subway. They saw young people knitting in NYC cafés. They noticed gorgeous yarn stores in Soho. The do-it-yourself (DIY) movement was flourishing in many categories—and that was, as they observed, extended to knitwear in the USA.

They both wondered "was this an opportunity?" When they returned to Spain, Alberto and Pepita confirmed that, in fact, knitting was still strictly the province of grandmothers in Europe. The available designs were not trendy. The yarn stores in Spain were neither trendy nor sophisticated. "Yes," they realized, "it IS an opportunity." It was their chance to make their day-dreams a day job.

Their research revealed that there were companies selling knitting kits, providing knitters with everything needed to knit a piece. Lightbulb #1 went on. This concept of "kits" could potentially broaden the audience for knitting. In addition to selling their high-quality and sustainably sourced yarns, they could make fashionable DIY kits (modern patterns packaged in simple but attractive kits), create seasons and other market segments (as in the fashion industry), and have unisex appeal. All encourage repeat business.

With Facebook still relatively new (2010) and Instagram not even in the Facebook womb, the would-be co-founders felt that they had a bit of time. Trends were then taking two to three years to make it from the US to Spain, and vice versa. Alberto and Pepita pilot-tested their idea with their PwC colleagues, asking them about their willingness to pay for a do-it-yourself product. The results of the pilot test were not great. In fact, they were the opposite of what the two were hoping to hear. Nonetheless, Alberto and Pepita were not dissuaded. They believed in their entrepreneurial vision and the DIY trend on the horizon. They knew it was time to take the leap.

Alberto and Pepita, still in their early twenties, quit their PwC jobs to "sell yarn on the Internet," much to their parents' chagrin and friends' surprise. As would-be entrepreneurs who left respected positions, Alberto and Pepita were considered trailblazers on their career journey. Entrepreneurship, particularly technology entrepreneurship, was blossoming in the United States, but not yet in Spain. There were few university programs, little venture capital, and no mentors for young entrepreneurs.

They believed in their idea fully and thought the timing was right for the idea and them personally. They concluded that with minimal responsibilities, no mortgages to pay, and no children to support, the worst-case scenario would be that they would fail and learn some big lessons along the way. Future jobs were possible, but this was an opportunity to create a life around a career they wanted.

They presented the We Are Knitters idea to their former university in Spain and won an entrepreneurial award. The small amount of money from the award was enough to start the company in 2010. We Are Knitters placed its first order of yarn in South America. The vision was a good one and the company grew from there. About a year and a half into starting We Are Knitters, Alberto and Pepita attracted investment from a couple of business angels and a small amount of private equity, followed by more rounds of investment in those initial stages of growth.

Alberto and Pepita mused that if there was a third co-founder, it would be the Internet. Technology, We Are Knitters' "silent partner," has enabled them to run almost the entire business virtually from Spain. This is critical as only about 5 percent of the company's revenues come from Spain; the other 95 percent come from countries outside Spain. Alberto, the company's creative director, notes that this would have been impossible without today's (or even 2010's) technology, including a website that's translated into different languages and the ability to easily ship orders almost worldwide. Today, We

Are Knitters remains almost entirely virtual, with selective collaborations with Anthropologie and Urban Outfitters, some big department stores, and pop-up stores in cities like Paris and New York.

Technology also aided in their marketing. The We Are Knitters name and brand practically jump off the web page, with an active and lively social media presence (particularly Instagram and Pinterest). There are various ways for knitters to increase their involvement with the brand, through referrals (earning We Are Knitters money), hosting or attending knitting parties, learning new techniques online, and participating in sponsored social causes.

And the icing on the cake for its fashion-loving founders: We Are Knitters has been written about in major fashion publications from *Elle* and *Glamour* to *Vogue*, as well as in business publications such as CNBC, the *Huffington Post*, and *Forbes*. This great publicity accelerated growth as articles were shared on social media.

The founders cite three main reasons for their success:

- They had an unwavering belief in their idea and didn't let anyone dissuade them. They believed in the trends they observed, and the vision inspired by those trends. *We Are Knitters* capitalized on and instantly became part of the DIY trend and the knitting trend.

- They stayed focused on their target market and product. For example, they've kept their product offerings simple and on target (DIY), instead of branching out into already-made items. This has provided inventory leverage because any one type of yarn can be used in multiple kits. They have extended their reach into other areas of DIY stitchery, such as crochet, embroidery and macrame.

- They were ambitious in their vision and courageous in the decisions they made. They made bold career moves and confident choices for future growth—even founding their Spanish company with an English name, anticipating their global reach.

When Alberto and Pepita describe what they nostalgically miss about working for an employer, they joke about missing office politics and having bosses (but noting that their investors, technically, are their bosses). More seriously, they share how being 100 percent committed to the business for ten years meant sacrificing a lot of their personal lives. Their work/life harmony "is changing for the better as the business and the team grow larger. Being embedded in the business conditioned our lives, for sure," says Alberto.

Finally, Alberto and Pepita offer some advice for those who would like to include entrepreneurship as a career act. First, they suggest that if you don't believe in your idea 100 percent, "just don't do it. You'll sacrifice a lot, and the investment might not pay off." Second, they highlight the importance of having a partner. When one partner is down, the other can be up. "As partners, you can work out the challenges together," notes Alberto.

Although Alberto and Pepita don't call themselves "the DIY entrepreneurs," they well could. They broke ground both in creating a new market (fashionable DIY knitting supplies and kits) and in creating a culture of technology entrepreneurship in Spain. Today, the founders spend time visiting universities and inspiring students with their story. They reached the "give-back" stage of their career journey much sooner than most.

And, most importantly, they love what they do. Like Alberto and Pepita did, we want you to craft a career journey so you too can say "you love what you do."

This chapter is dedicated to helping you understand your relationship with your career and the factors that can facilitate (or impede) your chances of career success. We want you to take the bold, ambitious, and courageous moves as Alberto and Pepita made. Starting a company like they did isn't right for everyone, but remaining in control and staying true to what you find satisfying and fulfilling is.

Some people remain locked in the invisible cage of an unfulfilling career, believing they lack control over their career destiny. They feel stuck, passively allowing others to control their relationship with work. This book is about self-managing your career. One meta-analysis (a statistical synthesis of the results from several academic research articles) found that people with more proactive personalities are more likely to actively manage their own careers and have greater career success and satisfaction than those who are more passive.[2]

If you are more proactive, you probably are naturally good at self-managing your career. You are more likely to seek out opportunities, advocate for yourself for developmental experiences, and actively change jobs to continue your growth. If this describes you, excellent! We hope this book helps you direct your high level of motivation to reach even further to your ideal career goal. If you are more passive, you are more likely to wait for the opportunities to come to you and might not embrace them when they do. For you, proactive career self-management might sound about as motivating as a root canal. If this describes you, we hope this book gives you the tools that make the activity seem less daunting and, hopefully, even feel empowering. Best of all, unlike a root canal, you won't need to avoid crunchy foods and rinse with salt water every day when you're done.

Even if you need to actively work at becoming more proactive, it is worth the effort. Another meta-analysis found that having a more proactive approach to career management is linked with greater career satisfaction.[3] These findings held true regardless of occupation, country, gender, age, and just about any other demographic characteristic that could apply to you. Career success. Career satisfaction. These are great career outcomes and, most would agree, worthwhile goals. We are here to tell you that they are within your reach.

Whether you are naturally proactive or need to work on it, career self-management has likely become a greater part of your work life. The playbook for career success has changed in recent years due to changes in the labor market, the rise of skill-based work, organizational restructuring, and the substitution of robots and artificial intelligence for jobs once done by people.[4] In this new reality, tenure is shorter, and companies are deploying employees' available skills more than developing their skills for the future.

When it comes to their employees' career flight paths, many companies have jumped from the plane and left you to land it. With less of a strategic need for companies to invest in all employees' professional development, career self-management has become essential.

Having a passive, not self-directed relationship with your career is like hanging on to an unrequited love. They can't give you what you need and holding on (hoping for something to change for the better) will just bring you heartache. It's over, mate. Move on. It is time to turn the page and have a relationship with your career that will love you back, so to speak. Like fostering any great relationship, crafting a great career is an active process that will require starting with a high level of self-awareness and honesty before making career decisions.

To set a strong foundation for this relationship, we ask you to start with some soul searching around each of the five indicators that can propel you toward (or hold you back from) your ideal career. They are:

1. Your Employer's Role in Managing Your Career

2. Your Role in Managing Your Career

3. Your Emotional Responses

4. Your Beliefs

5. Your Life's Circumstances

VISIT MYJOURNII.COM

Complete the assessment to create **your readiness dashboard**.

This assessment covers the five indicators discussed in this chapter that can either propel you toward or hold you back from your ideal career.

When all (or most) indicators on your dashboard are set to "green," your career journey will likely be a smoother and more enjoyable ride.

In each section, we ask you to be honest with yourself and try to identify which, if any, of these indicators will facilitate (or impede) you from taking control of your career journey. In fact, we want you to create a dashboard with five indicators, each resembling a traffic light illuminated either red, yellow, or green. At the end of this chapter, you will need to be honest with yourself. How many green lights do you have for your career journey?

Your goal from this chapter is to build awareness of each of these five indicators. Where possible, when an indicator is red or yellow, commit to an approach for moving the indicator to green. With all (or most) indicators set to green, your career journey can be a smoother and more enjoyable ride. Let's start the diagnostics, shall we?

Your employer's role in managing your career

Be honest. To what extent do you agree with any of the following sentences:

1. When evaluating my résumé, employers care more about where I have worked than the skills I have demonstrated.

2. Having a long tenure with my current employer will show my future employer that I am a committed and dedicated employee.

3. Larger organizations will manage my professional development better than smaller ones.

Did you agree with any of these? If Alberto and Pepita held even one of these beliefs, they would probably still be at PwC today, instead of enjoying their success with We Are Knitters. Each of these statements represents a dominant belief that propels people to work for well-known organizations rather than organizations that will position them well for their career journey. If you hold any of these beliefs, please keep reading.

The quote "insanity is doing the same thing, over and over again, but expecting different results" has been attributed to Benjamin Franklin, Albert Einstein, and Rita Mae Brown. Regardless of which luminary wrote it, the quote clearly describes today's most current career advice: to work for organizations that will "look good" on your résumés. The logic behind the advice suggests that "banner" organizations, such as those that appear on the Fortune 100 list, will have high-selection standards, more sophisticated career management programs, and better opportunities to be promoted. That might've been good advice fifty years ago, but today it fits the definition of insanity.

It is true that many banner organizations with great employer brands can differentially attract and retain great employees when they offer highly fulfilling work, developmental opportunities, and supportive organizational cultures. Research has found these best and brightest employees, in turn, improve the companies' financial performance.[5] But, for you as an employee, this will be a perfect symbiotic relationship *only* when your ideal career aligns with the work needed to create wealth in the company. A company will invest in your skills (i.e., you) when your skills are aligned with *the company's* strategic needs. Re-read that sentence a few times. It is critical in understanding your employer's role in your career. We'll wait.

––––––

When working for an employer, there are no opportunities to be an "undeclared major" or engage in soul-searching, company-sponsored self-discovery. Even the best and most progressive employee-centered companies will be paying you to use your skills and abilities. You might be on a path to career self-discovery, but your employer is **not** your sherpa. Most of the time, their bottom line doesn't align with your personal growth: your needs aren't on their balance sheet. The path is yours.

We hit this point hard because we want you to have the right relationship with your employer. We want you to be discerning about the type of experiences you will gain when working for an employer. We want you to be cautious about the promotions your employer will offer relative to the experiences you need to advance your career. It might be exciting to be offered the title of Very Important Head of Vital Stuff, but your interests lie elsewhere.

Steady promotions at banner companies once signaled that you have been selected into (and survived) the high standards of well-respected firms. In the past, this was enough because it provided job security. Job security was the goal in the past. But the job security of the past no longer exists in a world where the psychological contract between employers and employees has changed. Hanging onto this goal of employer commitment to job security has taken its toll. It has set many people up for career frustration as they handed their career control to their employers and found themselves downsized or sidelined. Workers hoping to stay in their jobs long enough to collect a gold watch are getting pink slips instead. They stopped driving, moved to the back seat, and ended up in a place they didn't want to go.

We want you to find an employer that aligns with your values and will support your professional development needed as you move along your career journey. This employer should have a strategic need for the skills you have today and those skills you hope to gain in the future while working there. This might mean ignoring the name of the company in favor of the skills you can gain while working there. Our advice to "ignore employer brand" and look for employers who will advance your career journey is *not* always easy to follow. Numerous research studies have found that people use corporate image and reputation as a quick way to judge the attractiveness of the employer.[6] This means that many people prefer to work for organizations representing the brands they know, trust, and respect. It's much easier to tell Mom, your spouse, or Aunt Gladys you've been hired by Consolidated International MegaFirm than it is to tell them you're going to start at Personal Wellness and Balance Synergies.

Always remember that your employer *can be* a source of career and life satisfaction but *is not responsible for* creating these in your life. Understanding this difference is critical for this mindset shift. We hope we can convince you throughout the book to leave this and other erroneous beliefs behind, to be more discerning when selecting career acts, and to follow an approach to have a more fulfilling relationship with your career.

You have a "green light" on this indicator when you prioritize the experiences you are gaining with an employer over the name of the company, and you understand that your employer is not responsible for your career self-discovery.

Your role in managing your career

Most people don't marry the first attractive person they meet on a dating app or at a salsa dancing meet-up. Over time, they learn what they value in a partner, meet a variety of people, become more discerning, and then possibly commit to a mutually loving relationship that enables them to flourish as a person. THEN they take a salsa dancing class together. Careers work the same way, minus the "until death do you part" part. Unfortunately, too many people become committed too quickly without discerning what they need in the context of their longer-term career journey. This has been a source of work dissatisfaction for many. Staying true to your goals and in control is needed to turn this around.

The Great Resignation has provided evidence that staying in control of your career will give you greater career satisfaction. With more people working from home and changing employers, employees had greater control over where and how they worked. With this heightened control, it is not surprising that The Conference Board noted the "changing dynamics of the relationship between employer and employee" and found:

> In 2020, overall job satisfaction remained historically high. Despite the pandemic, economic crisis, mass layoffs, and the increase in the unemployment rate, job satisfaction climbed from its lowest ever

rate of 42.6 percent recorded in 2010 to 56.9 percent—the highest in twenty years. The percentage of workers reporting engagement in their work also increased from 53.2 percent in November 2019 to 54.3 percent in November 2020.[7]

The extent to which you are in control of your career is, in part, based on your career adaptability, the extent to which you care about your career, control the decisions related to your career, explore career options with curiosity, and pursue options with confidence. Staying in control of your career means *taking some well-planned professional risks* based on your (real) talents, motivators, and values to confidently grow into increasingly more satisfying roles. It also means *knowing yourself,* your needs, and your motivations well enough to understand how you like to work and what engages you in your work. As Socrates said, "Know thyself, job-seeker, and you'll find a fulfilling career path." Maybe he only said the first part, but he certainly could've added the rest.

Achieving career control is worth it. In addition to greater job satisfaction, having greater career control and adaptability has many positive benefits for your life. A meta-analysis found that people who are higher in career adaptability had higher incomes, had better outcomes with their entrepreneurial ventures, and enjoyed higher life satisfaction overall.[8] Who wouldn't want these as part of their careers?

Consider the following ways to gain (or regain) greater control over your career:

- Have a positive mindset and don't allow yourself to settle for a mediocre career if you are motivated for a more fulfilling one. Keep moving, growing, and developing in the direction of your ultimate career goal. Great careers are a journey, not a destination. You will get what you settle for in your career (and in life).

- Do not relinquish control over your next career move to your manager or HR representative. They may be the nicest people in the office with the biggest candy bowls on their desks, but that doesn't mean they know your career hopes and dreams. Corporate career paths can be a path to nowhere unless the path is closely aligned with your discerning and self-directed career goals.

- Do not allow headhunters to determine your next move. While it's flattering to be tapped for a bigger job, this is a bad career strategy unless the step is exactly the one you were seeking independently. "Career management by headhunter" keeps you doing more of what you have already done well without too much (if any) developmental stretch. Remember that you are not the headhunter's client. The head-hunter's client is the company that needs your skill set. The headhunter looks great to have a perfect candidate. *Perfect* for the company might quickly mean little developmental opportunity for you.

- Stay in control of timing for when you change roles or engage in professional development. Shift strategically (not emotionally) from one secure position to another more interesting, developmental, and fulfilling one. Stay in control by changing jobs before you are forced to do so by your employer.

- Communicate your professional interests to your managers. It might be the case that your ideal career *is* with your current employer. Unless you convey your interests, your career goals will remain invisible to those who can help you achieve them. Effective people-leaders know that their role is to balance your skills and interests with the company needs. The next best role might be where you are.

- Don't waste time hoping for a change in a current unfulfilling work situation if you have no reason to believe things will change. Numerous research suggests that clicking your heels together and saying "There's no place like my dream job" won't work. Well, there is no real research on heel-clicking, but we do know that bad situations rarely change into great ones.

- We know that change is hard for most people but don't be afraid to change careers, especially when the move is well thought-out and well planned. Great careers involve some risk and information, and planning lowers that risk.

You'll know you have a "green light" on this indicator when you have a deep sense that you, and not your employer, are in control of your career. You are active in your career development: you have a career goal, a plan for the next phase, and are proactively working toward your ideal career.

Your emotional responses

You selected this book for a reason that is unique to you. Perhaps you were looking for a way to strategically channel your high energy and motivation for your career. Or, perhaps, you are seeking some insight to reignite a stalled career. More likely, you have a nagging feeling that there is more out there.

From wherever you start, the thought of a career change can produce a swirl of emotions such as fear, doubt, and anxiety mixed with excitement, anticipation, and a sense of euphoria at the thought of starting something new. You might feel all these emotional responses. You might feel some of them. You might feel none of them.

We invite you to bring whatever authentic responses you have to these pages as you interact with the exercises and ideas. We only ask that they are yours, not responses you believe you should feel. Too often work-related changes are associated with prescribed feelings that don't square with our reality. Maybe you have heard one of these: "You must be excited to be graduating and starting your career." "You must be nervous to be leaving a company you were with for twenty years." "You must be ready to move on." Please ignore anything that sounds like one of these prepackaged attributions. Letting other people tell you what feelings you're having is like using the Magic 8 Ball to make serious life choices for you. If you are too young to remember the Magic 8 Ball, then imagine asking Chat GPT to plan your career. The only feelings you *must* feel about a career decision are those you are *actually* having.

Staying in touch with your true emotional responses will propel you to ask more questions and seek information to make better decisions, explore atypical options, seek new skills, and the like. If your gut feeling is that something doesn't feel right, it probably isn't. Keep looking. Again, do not allow society or kindly Aunt Gladys to dictate to you what you "should be" feeling. Emotions happen in a context—but the context is yours to interpret without allowing it to be interpreted for you.

Articulating your actual emotional responses is not as easy as it might seem because we all live in socialized culture bubbles that value certain career choices over others. In other words, many of us are shaped, cajoled, convinced, or subtly socialized into preferring certain careers over others. Unintentionally, being socialized into career choices while ignoring gut feelings can keep many away from their most fulfilling careers. When it comes to career choices, connecting with your emotional truth requires some practice. To build this skill, try these:

- **Be precise when you name the feeling you are experiencing and the reason for that feeling.** For example, "I'm excited about starting the new job" might more precisely be "I'm excited to start with a company that has a higher-energy culture and I look forward to developing new technical skills." This precision gives you a better guide on your career needs; In this case, the precision is that you "value a high-energy culture" and "skill development."

- **Identify conflicting and pervasive feelings as valid because they provide valuable information.** Continuing from the previous example, ". . . While I am energized by this new opportunity, I will miss the daily interactions with my close work friends." The conflicting feelings give you relative information: that you value the combination of high-energy culture and skill development *over* working with friends (just don't tell your friends you feel that way).

- **Remember that emotion can be fleeting**. At your going-away party, you might have a deep sense of loss and sadness leaving your work friends. Isolate that feeling (again, by being precise). On the night of the party, you might say: "It was tough to say good-bye to familiar colleagues and I might miss seeing regularly a few close work friends." Check in again with your emotional responses a few months later. It might be the case that you are happy to have stayed in touch with two close friends from your previous job but really don't miss everyone as much as you thought you would.

Even if you have a high level of self-awareness about your emotional responses and feelings about your career, you might still experience career limitations because you have an intolerance of ambiguity. Some people truly fear change. Minimally, as humans, we tend not to like it very much. That said, the most successful people we know fear settling *more* than they fear change. They dislike complacency *more* than they dislike ambiguity.

We all vary with respect to our comfort level with change and ambiguity. As an individual difference, it really is not fair for us to offer pithy suggestions in the hopes of turning the most cautious reader into a career bungee jumper. If you really dislike your job (slightly more than you dislike change), we suggest not changing a thing in your current work situation—but, rather, add a small additional career act, rooted in something you love (more on that in upcoming chapters). You can then control when and how (and if ever) your job will change by dedicating more time to this additional career act. When you feel comfortable and the change no longer produces anxiety, you'll make the leap.

You'll know you have a "green light" on this indicator when you have a high level of self-awareness of your honest emotional reactions to work and your level of comfort (or fear) with changing your current work situation.

Your beliefs

"I hate my job." These words are soul-crushing to hear, let alone experience. *Have you ever uttered them?* If so, we hope it was to yourself, with a friend over a beer, and not during a meeting with your supervisor. You're not alone if you feel you are toiling in an unfulfilling job now, with the only hope of someday retiring to start living a more-fulfilling life. The assumption on which the concept of retirement is based—that we need to defer our life's happiness until we reach our senior years—is unfortunate and growing increasingly more illogical with every passing year, especially among those who enjoy what they do.

This retirement-oriented, delayed-fulfillment belief about career malaise is as outdated today as your VCR and CD player (if you are old enough to remember what those are). At this stage we are just doing some diagnostics. Understanding the role of your beliefs for staying in an unfulfilling job can help you identify the sources of resistance you might need to overcome first before you start your career journey.

Consider some different beliefs about work for a minute: At one extreme, there are the *life-is-too-short-to-be-unhappy-at-work* folks. They have a belief that they should be happy with whatever they opt to do for a living. Career conversations with people at this end of the continuum tend to be more creative, self-directed, and solution-focused. At the other extreme, there are the *yes-I-hate-my-job-but-that-is-why-they-call-it-work* folks. They want to get out of the rut but believe that this is where they need to remain. They tend to believe in an outdated employment scenario and are more pessimistic about exploring options. Career conversations with people at this end of the continuum tend to be depressing.

This latter end of the continuum sheds light on the beliefs, often rooted in cognitive biases, that keep people in unfulfilling jobs. Check if you hold any of these:

- **Scarcity.** *"I cannot change jobs now; I make too much money and it would be impossible to find something at my level."* Really? Is it "impossible" to find something at your level? People who hold a scarcity mindset believe that they need to hold onto their job because there aren't any viable options out there. If this is your belief, you are in a mental game of musical chairs: you believe there won't be a seat for you when the music stops. If you have this belief, remember that job changes are not an "all or nothing" risk. You can explore options to test your assumption about whether alternatives exist. You can plan and prepare for a change. There is no need to leave before you are ready. Also, if you hold this mindset, remember that staying in a job is not a guarantee that you will be employed in the future. (See "your needs aren't on their balance sheet," previously mentioned.)

- **Loss aversion.** *"I only have two more years before I am fully vested in the pension program. I can suffer through anything for a few more years."* The human resources practices designed to encourage retention often work. This is great news for companies hoping to lower their costs associated with voluntary turnover and unwanted exits. They work effectively because of a natural human tendency called loss aversion. This means that we respond to losses more powerfully than we do equivalent financial gains. For example, walking away from your $5,000 annual bonus will register more painfully than starting a new job that is offering you a $5,000 hiring bonus. There is a magnetic draw holding us in place if we believe we will lose money.

- **Escalation of commitment (or misplaced loyalty).** *"I have worked in this profession for fifteen years, I am not about to give up the years I have put in to start over." "I have given a lot of myself to this organization."*

28

Humans naturally want to justify the things they have spent time and effort in. It is a common belief to stay committed to a job beyond what is warranted. Remember that your employer owns "your" job; you do not. There are no guarantees that "your" job will be there in the future, just as there is no expectation that you will stay with the organization if there is a better opportunity for you elsewhere. There are no gold stars for attendance in this stage of your life. Understand your beliefs for remaining in a role and whether they were formed from an escalation of commitment.

- **Pessimism.** *"It is naïve to think you can like what you do." "I do not believe there are any fulfilling jobs—work is called 'work' for a reason."* Unless you are a natural pessimist, the underlying belief that there are "no fulfilling options" is usually related to a lack of creativity for what those options could be. This book should help with that and, if you fall into this pessimistic category, we'd suggest you start talking to people who genuinely seem to enjoy what they do for a living. They exist and their careers might motivate you to be more optimistic about your career.

A "green light" on this dimension means you have awareness of and control over the cognitive biases that shape your beliefs about work. You have positive beliefs in your approach to your career journey. You are confident, have high self-efficacy, and are optimistic about a better future. You have everything you need to get what you want (except for the other important things we're going to cover in this book).

Your life's circumstances

Your great career will not be built by simply wishing you were in a different reality, one where time and money was unlimited. We need to be honest about the circumstances affecting our careers, such as the commitments you have to your loved ones. Few people live in a career bubble, one in which their decisions will have no effect on others' lives. Begin by asking yourself honestly: *Who will be directly affected by your career choices—and how?*

If you are a single person without a family to support or someone with a securely employed partner who can easily cover family bills during the time of transition, you may have more flexibility with your career choices. If this is your enviable position, use that freedom wisely for as long as you have it to progress quickly and deliberately toward an ultimate career goal.

Your career decisions might have implications for your spouse, partner, family, and loved ones—especially if you are responsible, even in part, for your family income. Be open with those who will be influenced in your career decisions and discuss, for example:

- **Debt.** For many people, their debt shapes the decisions they make. The reality of debt has a powerful influence on the career choices we make. For example, new college graduates who are in debt might need to accept a job that will enable them to pay for their student loans. Similarly, those who take on large mortgages will also select career opportunities to pay that expense. If you are overextended financially, work to address this first. Try to get your personal finances under control so you can mentally give yourself license to make career-related choices that are both financially rewarding and fulfilling. While you're doing that, you can loan this book to a friend—if they promise to return it when you're ready.

- **Savings and loans.** You might be in a situation where you will take out a loan or use your or your family's savings to start a business or to invest in self-development (e.g., a degree or a training course). If you are solo, this is a personal risk. If you are in a committed relationship and partners have a different tolerance for risk, the use of family funds for career advancement can cause friction. One way to address this is to set a limit on how much risk can be tolerated and a collective approach for evaluating milestones for investing more. Another strategy is for partners to alternate the investment in their career. For example, one person completes a degree after which the other person takes time to start a side business.

- **Time.** As your career builds, you might be in a situation where you have less time for your loved ones because of the time you will be investing in your career. Instead of giving up time with loved ones, we encourage you to become relentlessly protective of your time. To do this, pull back on other non-career activities to make the time needed for your loved ones while building your career. In some cases, it might mean you need to grow your career more slowly due to family commitments. In other cases, it might mean saying "bye-bye" to binge watching your favorite series or your trivia night for a period while you work on your career.

- **Relocation.** You might need to relocate for your career. Start early having relocation conversations with loved ones and include those age-appropriate family members who will be influenced by the decision, when possible. In some cases, you will need to remain in a certain geographic location for the sake of your loved ones.

We cannot prescribe what is right for you and your partner or family. We do suggest having an open discussion regarding how your career options could affect them and try to seek a compromise that enables forward momentum without causing too much anxiety or stress on those you love. A clear "green light" on this indicator exists when you understand the role that your life circumstances will play in your career. The green light isn't when you eliminate them (except for debt, if possible). The green light is when you have clarity and agreement around their boundaries. With this green light, you will know how much debt, risk, time, and distance you can incur for the sake of your career.

KEY TAKEAWAYS

- Understand that your employer is not responsible for your career self-discovery and career advancement. You are.

- Take ownership of your career by maintaining control over your career decisions. Remain active in your career development: have a career goal, a plan for the next phase, and be proactive in working toward your ideal career.

- Understand your true emotional responses about career decisions and your level of comfort with (or fear of) career changes. Build self-awareness and an approach for managing negative emotions.

- Identify your beliefs affecting your career journey. Have an awareness of and control over the cognitive biases that shape your beliefs about work, such as a scarcity mentality, loss aversion, and escalation of commitment. Cultivate optimism.

- Understand your life's circumstances. Everyone is bound to the reality of life and those realities and responsibilities need to be honored as you craft your career. Be sure to have clarity and agreement around their boundaries.

CHAPTER 2

GAIN SELF-AWARENESS OF YOUR TALENTS

I think self-awareness is probably the most important thing towards being a champion.
—BILLIE JEAN KING

With an early interest in computers and electrical engineering (and with a genetic predisposition to starting small businesses, he jokes), Omer Trajman began working in middle school.[1] He started with magic shows for kids' parties and progressed into tech support and QA jobs for technology companies—not your traditional kids' summer jobs or internships.

Armed with a new BSc in computer engineering, he pursued a career in software development, starting a company for product development at age twenty-two ("which went nowhere") and then joining a few other companies.

At age twenty-seven, Omer took a software development position in the Boston area with a promising, venture-capital-backed start-up company, as one of its founding engineers. This turned out to be pivotal for his career and his life. Within a year or so, it became evident to the company's leadership that he was not a good software engineer. But he was *very* good at finding bugs and talking to customers and others about the technology and how to use it. To their credit, his bosses recognized his talent and created a role for him: field engineer. He went on to build out the field engineering team, hiring dozens of people as well as coming up with new product ideas emerging from his contacts with customers and partners.

In his thirties, Omer was recruited by a partner company in Silicon Valley to join as their first VP. There, he felt he could rapidly expand his experience, opportunity, and contacts. He repeated his previous success in a new company based on open-source software and cloud computing, two hot industry trends. He and his colleagues went on to start a spin-off software company, his second time as a founder.

At this point, as it often does, serendipity came into play. Out of both practicality (the varying geographic locations of the founders) and necessity (the high cost of hiring good talent and office space in the Bay Area), Omer and his co-founders asked: "What if we deploy the open-source (distributed) method of creating software to how you run a company?"

The distributed company concept enabled Omer to move his family back to the Boston area, to bucolic Vermont (a life goal). And the model *worked*: by the time the founders sold the company, it had employees working remotely from twenty states. Although initially "a bit weird" for the company's investors, the distributed-workplace model was beloved by employees. The acquiring company (which initially had been opposed to continuing the model) eventually turned to Omer and team for advice on using it to run their global company.

As we write this, Omer is in his early forties. He's used his bi-coastal technology field-engineer "cred" and unique client-whisperer skills in founding several other companies. He also serves as an advisor and investor to other companies and is a member of the Derby Entrepreneurship Center advisory board at his alma mater, Tufts, which helps students become citizens who make lasting impacts through entrepreneurship. Those bosses who helped him recognize his unique skill and put him on the right path are lifelong mentors.

Omer's career path was consistently defined by intentionality: first, becoming self-aware of his strengths (with the help of an employer) then intentionally picking opportunities that leveraged those unique strengths (at the intersection of technology and business) and intentionally steering toward his personal goals of work/life harmony.

His path could *never* have been defined by an HR person and rarely could be recognized in a rigid corporate career structure dictated by promotional gateways. Mentorship and enlightened talent management—from his first employer—played a pivotal role as did serendipity and his natural grit and curiosity.

Omer is one of approximately 162 million Americans working in the US labor force today. The experience each one has with work varies tremendously, with people like Omer being at one end of that continuum, engaged and fulfilled. At the other end, sits roughly 15 percent of workers who report having *miserable* work experiences and are fully disengaged, according to Gallup estimates.[2] It is not surprising that McKinsey's 2021 "Great Attrition or Great Attraction" study found about 40 percent of employees are at least "somewhat likely" to leave their current job, noting that:

> Employees are tired, and many are grieving. They want a renewed and revised sense of purpose in their work. They want social and interpersonal connections with their colleagues and managers. They want to feel a sense of shared identity. . . . They want meaningful—though not necessarily in-person—interactions, not just transactions.[3]

You can hear a collective career frustration embedded in the survey's sentiment. At a time of the Great Opportunity, the sense of career dissatisfaction is especially disheartening. We can do better. Throughout your adult years, prior to retirement, you will spend almost half your waking hours in work-related activities. If you spend forty-five years of your life working, you will have, on average, 241 workdays each year and each of those days will include 8.7 hours of actual work for 2,097 hours of work each year. *What sane person would want to be unhappy or unfulfilled for 2,097 hours each year?* No one (we hope).

Unfortunately, when many people make job changes, they often do so to move *away from* a bad work situation, rather than *toward* a career goal. When this is the case, they often end up unfulfilled once the thrill of the new job wears off. This reality is called hedonic adaptation, an exciting burst of dopamine for the new experience that fades when it becomes part of our reality. If you don't believe us, think of the last new car or smartphone you bought. Think of the first few months after moving into a new city or the first few months with a new lover. All of these have one thing in common: they are exciting at first but the excitement fades as they become part of our daily reality. The same thing happens at a new job: once the excitement of having the key to the employee washroom wears off, people log back on to ineedanewjobnow.com.

We see signs of this every day. According to a Yahoo Finance/Harris Poll, about 40 percent of employees are considering changing jobs, with over 80 percent of them planning to make the move in the next six months.[4] *Are you one of them?* If your job change is not well-planned, directed toward your ultimate career goal, you are riding a Ferris Wheel of hedonic adaptation, a vicious, perpetual job change cycle. Think of it as Groundhog Day, vocational version. The new job will feel great when it starts, but will lose its luster when it becomes routine, exposing inevitable flaws. Pretty soon you're waking up with the identical feeling of dread you felt before you'd go into work at your last job. While getting out of an unsatisfying work situation is a good thing, we believe you deserve more—far more—than consecutive jobs that will quickly become uninteresting when the novelty wears off.

We want your next job to be a strategic move getting you closer to your most fulfilling career. To that end, the goal of this chapter is to help you out of this vicious cycle of lackluster career moves—and get you into a virtuous one. The bonus: you can still enjoy all the dopamine buzzes along the way. And they won't disappear before your six-month review. We promise.

Finding your career goal and mapping the journey to get there requires some self-awareness about your talents, motivators, and preferences for your career. In this chapter, we'll share ways to uncover them. We hope you will be able to identify what you want (and don't want) from your ideal career and the career acts needed to leverage your talents, satisfy your motivations, and live a more fulfilling life. As you work through this chapter, we invite you to complete the exercises found on www.myJournii.com. We hope the exercises will help you build self-awareness and identify:

1. What puts you into a state of flow

2. Your natural talents

3. Your best work environment

4. Your career needs and motivators

5. What you don't want in your career

Identify what puts you in a state of flow

It was Confucius who said, "Choose a job you love, and you will never have to work a day in your life." He chose the job of coming up with brilliant pearls of wisdom that people would be quoting for thousands of years, and he never regretted that choice. Confucius's advice to follow our passions is as true today as it was 2,500 years ago. In doing so, you lose yourself in your work, which feels effortless and enjoyable.

This sense of being fully absorbed in and hyper-focused on what you are doing has been coined the state of "flow" by psychologist Mihály Csíkszentmihályi.[5] Unique to each of us, very diverse things can place us into a state of flow, such as solving the day's Wordle, playing an intense video game, cooking a new recipe, or having great sex.

You will likely reach a state of flow when you are experiencing an optimal challenge (neither too easy nor too difficult) which produces an ideal level of stimulation and is something inherently rewarding. Think about playing Wordle, a video game, or cooking (we'll leave sex out of this example). If you enjoy one of these activities but the challenge is too easy, you might be bored. At the other extreme, if it is too challenging, you might become frustrated. But when your skills meet the task at hand for an engaging challenge, you can find flow.

For many people, when they achieve flow they "just know" because they are awash with intrinsic reward from the activity in which they are engaged. If you are accustomed to practicing mindfulness, you will not be surprised to learn that the feeling of mindfulness (i.e., a non-judgmental awareness of being fully present) is associated with higher levels of flow.[6] When you are in a state of flow, you are in the moment. The features of flow identified by Csíkszentmihályi are:

1. A sense of intense and focused concentration where you were "lost" in whatever task you were doing.

2. A sense of sublime pleasure that made you feel more alive and connected.

3. A sense of clarity for what needs to be accomplished and how to accomplish it.

4. A sense of joy in doing the task.

5. A sense that you are in control and have what it takes to succeed in the task.

6. A sense of tranquility, without worry or anxiety.

7. Losing all sense of time, feeling lost in the moment.

What a great list! Who wouldn't want more of these, more often? We can make an educated guess that your current job isn't coming close to fulfilling most (or any) of the features on this list. Beyond just a positive buzz, research has found that achieving a state of flow has benefits related to positive well-being, health, functioning, and engagement. Not surprisingly, flow is considered one of the hallmarks of the state of happiness and is central for a fulfilling career. We want you to select career acts that place you into a state of flow as much as possible.

Everyone reaches flow in different ways. What creates a state of flow for you might be something another person finds boring or anxiety producing. For example, Andy tends to work multiple projects simultaneously. Working with their collective intellectual energy places him into a state of flow. When inspired, he also drills down deeply into one project for a few hours, days, or even weeks. Like Andy, Paula can lose herself in a single engaging project, such as writing or conducting data analyses for a research study. Unlike Andy, when Paula tries to work on multiple projects simultaneously, she feels unproductive rather than energized. Everyone achieves their state of flow differently.

Identifying the types of tasks that put you into a state of flow will be extremely helpful in building self-awareness about the features your ideal career should include. To identify what puts you in a state of flow, try the following:

1. Begin by naming the ten activities you do most in a typical week. List them in the following chart.

2. For each activity, using the "very frequently" to "never" scale that follows, rate the extent to which the task produces the following feelings of (1) losing track of time, feeling engaged and absorbed, (2) being energized, happy, and motivated, and (3) feeling confident, creative, and cognitively stimulated.

3. Calculate the total for each activity.

4. Among those with the highest scores, what is common among them? Does a pattern emerge? For example, are those with the highest scores when you are working alone? Communicating with colleagues? Being creative? Organizing?

5. Spend time analyzing your patterns. Repeat the exercise with new activities whenever you sense a new activity brought you to that state of flow.

5– Very Frequently

4– Frequently

3– Occasionally

2– Rarely

1– Very Rarely

0– Never

List work-related tasks:	When I do this task, I lose track of time, feel engaged and absorbed.	When I do this task, I feel energized, happy, and motivated.	When I do this task, I feel confident, creative, and cognitively stimulated.	TOTAL
1				
2				
3				
4				
5				
6				
7				
8				
9				
10				

Once you can identify the types of activities that put you into a state of flow, you can identify the types of jobs for which that activity is needed. For example, if you enjoy being creative, perhaps your ideal career is in graphic design, advertising, or writing. If you love communicating, maybe you would be an effective trainer, counselor, or teacher. *Can you connect what puts you into a state of flow with your natural talents in the next section?*

Identify your natural talents

Do you know what your natural talents are? If you are like most people, the answer is "I don't know." Talent is a bit like that proverbial piece of marble before a sculptor begins to chisel. Like the chiseled statue, your talents are "in you": reflection and experience will help them emerge and become more refined, but they will likely need effort to uncover. Thankfully, we can offer tools to help that don't involve any hammers or razor-sharp chisels.

Your talents are not your current job, your university major, an occupational category, or even the job title you hope to occupy someday. They are the skills and abilities that come most naturally to you, the things that you excel in faster than most people.

If you are like most people, you might not even realize you have a talent until someone helps you see it. This was certainly the case for both of us. Paula was an embarrassingly bad writer throughout her university career. Her grad school advisor once told her that a paper she wrote (which she thought was decent) looked like someone threw commas at the paper and left them wherever they landed. Fair enough. At that time, she didn't have the skills of a writer but, as she later learned, she did have a talent to create and disseminate social science findings in an accessible and useful way. Her natural talent was for creative and straightforward explanation. Once she began the process of learning the skills of writing and speaking, she excelled faster than others as a "pracademic" writer.

Andy has a natural talent "seeing" the intersection of computers and humans. He has always enjoyed making machines function gracefully with people and learned that it was a unique talent early in his career. In fact, he first discovered his talent when writing computer games in high school. He learned this was a natural talent as he excelled faster than others in programming at an early age.

As noted, Socrates gave us the sage advice approximately 2,500 years ago to "know thyself." This is especially useful advice when uncovering your natural talents. To uncover your talents, engage with as many of the following exercises as possible. Don't be shy in asking those who know you for their insight on some of these. Take your time with these exercises to gain the greatest level of self-awareness. This is an important step. It is worth the investment of time. As Socrates might've said, "Knowing thyself is a process that takes a little longer than just filling in a quiz on the Internet to find out what kind of tree you'd be if you were a tree."

REFLECT ON YOUR MOMENTS OF PRIDE

This might feel a bit odd at first but try to list between five and ten moments in your life where you can recall feeling a sense of pride. You know you've identified one if it is something you like to share with others or if it is something that gives you an inner sense of accomplishment. Andy is proud of co-founding Vertica, especially when he and the team were acquiring their first customers. One of their early adopters was Facebook, which had a VERY high bar in terms of technology. Facebook's CIO announced public praise for Vertica, stating that Vertica excelled in the results-oriented and innovative high demands that Facebook placed on it.

Hearing the praise from this demanding client helped Andy see how much he thrived in high-performance environments. This feature remains core to how he manages his career and his companies today. For Paula, she is proud of her biweekly segment on CNN called "Reclaim Your Career." The insight here was that she flourished in situations where she could make solid social science research valuable to many. To this day, she is at her best when teaching, keynoting, writing, and creating professional development sessions.

Your moments of pride might be achievements that took time (like growing a company or having a TV segment) or brief moments (like receiving a great grade on an exam or helping a friend solve a computer problem). They might be from your youth or adulthood, work-related or nonwork related. Whenever and wherever they originate, your moments of pride will help you identify situations when you know your effort was "worth it." They will, as a group, provide some deeper insight into your underlying characteristics and abilities that will shine when you are at your best.

We asked some colleagues for their moments of pride. They shared:

- "The moment I arrived in Dubai for my first international assignment when I was in my early thirties. I wanted an experience in another country and worked hard to be selected for the opportunity even though I was young for the job." (This person is adventurous and ambitious and is now a senior global leader in an international company.)

- "The day my short story was released as part of a nonfiction compilation. It was the first time I saw my work in print." (This person is highly creative and expressive and is now a science fiction novelist.)

- "When I was in high school, I led an effort to raise money for a homeless shelter." (This person is empathetic and persistent and is now a grant writer for a large nonprofit.)

- "In college, I fixed an elderly neighbor's car that would not start. Her gratitude was rewarding but I had fun trying to figure it out and fix it." (This person is analytical and curious and is now an engineer.)

- "My wedding was a source of pride. We had such a tight budget, but it was a beautiful and fun event. I loved seeing the small details come together." (This person is detail-oriented and organized and is now a project manager.)

You can give this exercise a try.

1. List five to seven experiences from your past that have been the most positive for you, focusing on the experiences that gave you the greatest sense of pride. Usually, the things that are sources of pride give you little hits of dopamine or pleasure when you think about them. They can be from your early life, personal life, education, or career. As you select them, try to focus on how you feel as you recall them.

2. For each experience, try to name up to five personal traits you felt you used (or others would observe in you) during this experience. Examples of traits are persistence, ambition, curiosity, kindness, independence, empathy, diplomacy, creativity, confidence, and charisma. There are hundreds of other traits, so you'll need to take some time with this.

3. For each experience, try to name up to three reasons this was a source of pride for you. Examples of reasons are phrases such as: overcame adversity, made it myself, created community, was the leader, impressed others that mattered to me, and was the first to do it.

4. Last, try to name up to three skills or abilities you were using to achieve this. Examples of skills and abilities include counseling, engineering, problem-solving, writing, teaching, coordinating, presenting, etc.

5. Pencils down. Now the fun part. Is there any consistency when reading across the words you wrote for each of your five to seven examples? If so, you are likely identifying the descriptions of situations that would put you into a state of flow. If not, keep reading.

ASK THOSE WHO KNOW YOU BEST

Sometimes the best way to understand our talents is to ask those who know us well. They might see the things that we cannot. If you are comfortable doing this, sometimes the direct approach is the best one: You can ask a diverse group of trusted people in your circle to help you identify your talents. Include people from different domains of your life, such as family members, friends, teammates, mentors, and coworkers. Include people who know you well, who do not have an agenda for directing your career in a certain direction, and who don't have a vested interest in you staying in your current role.

Asking your boss might result in an answer like, "You're good at everything. Now get back to work." Spending time with each person independently (this is not a group project), ask the person:

- What do you think I do exceptionally well?
- Do I have a unique skill that you have observed?
- How would you describe my skills and abilities?
- What talent do you think I possess but do not utilize enough?
- Is there a profession you could see me in, other than the one I am in currently?

There is a more formal version of this exercise that Paula uses whenever she teaches her MBA course in global leadership. Her students complete a semester-long project called the "Reflected Best Self-Portrait," a well-researched personal development approach developed by academics from the University of Michigan and Harvard Business School.[7] It is used globally in business schools and organizations to help people understand their talents. To conduct this exercise:

1. Identify ten to fifteen people from different parts of your life. Paula's students will usually include a mix of the following: their partner or spouse; parents and grandparents; aunts and uncles; cousins; former teachers; mentors; religious guides; coaches; professors with whom they worked closely; friends from childhood, high school, college, graduate school; teammates; coworkers; and, when appropriate, past (or current) managers. Pets don't count. Double-blind studies show that their data is frequently unreliable.

2. Invite each person to provide short descriptions of between one and three stories of what you were doing at the time when they observed you at your very best. Ask everyone at once. Give them a deadline (about three weeks) and send reminders along the way. It is always

good to ask more than ten to fifteen people because some people will just be too busy or forget.

3. If you have the willpower, do not read them as they come in. Wait to read them at the same time. Mark your calendar for a day to do the analysis. On that day, set aside a few hours to read through the stories people wrote. Have a pen and paper ready. Make yourself a cup of tea or pour a glass of wine. Find a comfy chair in a quiet location and start reading.

4. Read the stories through once without taking notes. Read them through again to see if the first pattern or theme emerges. Repeat this a few more times until you have identified all the themes. Please note that this is an eye-opening and beautiful experience for many of Paula's students. Even one of her most unemotional students admitted to shedding some happy tears as he read that his grandma, baseball coach from high school, cousin, fiancé, and current classmate all saw the same strengths of patience, resilience, and an ability to rally others when they are down.

5. Think through those themes and use them to identify your talents. Then, think about how your talents could be used on your career journey. Is your ideal career one in which your best, most talented self will emerge most often?

TAKE ASSESSMENT TESTS

You've tried introspection. You've asked others. Are you still not sure about your natural skills and abilities—and the situations that would put you into a state of flow? That is OK because there are countless websites happy to help with self-assessment. In fact, the Internet is full of "tests" to assess your personality based on everything from your vegetable preferences to your favorite ice cream flavor. Although these might be entertaining, they are neither useful nor valid (except if they tell you that you like kale, which is useful to know).

TAKE AN INTEREST PROFILER TO EXPLORE CAREERS

Visit: www.mynextmove.org.

At this site, you can search careers with key words, browse careers by industry, and (our favorite) take an interest profiler assessment and receive suggestions for possible careers that match your interests.

O*NET Interest Profiler is sponsored by the US Department of Labor, Employment & Training Administration, and developed by the National Center for O*NET Development.

It is an outstanding resource available to anyone—for free.

We are passionate about having you craft your ideal career and doing so on a solid foundation of self-awareness for your strengths. In fact, this was so important to us that we co-founded a public benefit corporation called Skiilify, which enables you to access assessment tools for free. You can check out myJournii.com for career diagnostics and myGiide.com. The latter is helpful if you work in a multicultural environment (as many people do today) as it gives you a chance to self-assess your values and cultural agility competencies. We also strongly recommend using other valid and free resources, such as the O*NET Interest Profiler (see text box). And remember, the Ouija Board is for entertainment purposes only.

If you find other tests online that look promising, please evaluate their efficacy before wasting your time or money. Consider the following:

1. What entity is marketing or promoting the test or assessment tool? If it is a reputable organization, association, or institution, it is probably (but not always) an effective tool. Reputable organizations will

promote tools with scientific evidence, especially if they list research published in peer-reviewed scientific journals.

2. Are any of the psychometric properties of the test given, such as reliability or validity? Both reliability and validity are critical test attributes on which assessment tools or tests should be judged. These tell us whether a test is an accurate measure of a given skill or ability (reliability) and whether the test scores relate to an external measure of performance (validity).

3. Was the result of the test consistent with the feedback you have received from others about your knowledge, skills, and abilities— or about what you know to be true about your knowledge, skills, and abilities?

ENGAGE A CAREER COUNSELOR

If you would like more one-on-one guidance, you might be interested in seeking out a qualified career counselor who is trained in asking the right questions to guide you to your self-awareness for your career decisions. Most career counselors will have you work through assessment tests and then discuss the interpretation of the scores and how they apply to your career situation and goals.

If you have access, many colleges have career counseling departments, and some professional organizations provide career counseling services for a reasonable fee. You can also access professional career counselors who work independently. As a word of caution, please ask for references and contact those references to learn more about any given counselor's effectiveness. The field is currently full of certifications but is not regulated, which means that anyone is able to "hang a shingle" as a career planner, career coach, or career advisor. If you find a website for a "certifyde carere counsiller dude" keep looking. If you need some suggestions for career counselors, follow us on social media where we profile the work of great career counselors.

Identify your best work environment

Do you have a general idea of the environment in which you are the happiest working? Some people can answer this question easily, without even knowing what they would like to do within that environment. As an example, Paula likes to be alone in a quiet cocoon of solitude to engage in any creative task, like writing. The same level of quiet Paula cherishes would be maddening for Andy, a person who appreciates a high-energy environment, who has his best meetings at popular restaurants.

Appreciating the differences in how people want to configure their work environments to suit their preferences, Andy created a new approach to the work environment at his company Tamr. Tamr starts with *Digital First*, enabling everyone to work digitally, first and foremost. Secondly, Tamrs work *Primarily Remote*. Many Tamrs prefer to work remotely, so Tamr gives teams a budget to use as they see fit to collaborate. Some Tamrs use their budget to get together for monthly off-sites, some for WeWork space. Each team gets to choose its preference. Tamr also has physical space for onboarding, which Andy and the Tamrs have found is much more effective when done in person.

Since your work environment will affect your overall satisfaction, it is important to assess your tangible preference for how you best like to work. Maybe you have declared something like the following: "I could never work a desk job," or "I like the energy of a small start-up company," or "I like working with my hands." If you have made a statement like these, they are your clear preferences for the tangible aspects of your work environment. These statements describe your environment but do not necessarily describe what you are doing. For example, "I could never work a desk job" could be uttered by a professional football player or a tour guide at a national park. "I like to work with my hands" could be conveyed by an orthopedic surgeon or a house painter.

For some people, the *tangible environment* in which they work, the way they interact with and move in their physical space, is a non-negotiable factor of their ideal career and the career acts along the way. For others, it is a secondary preference. To get a better sense for your preferences, consider the possible options and identify any of those in which you have a strong preference.

1. Working with physical movement:
   a. Do you prefer being in motion, either using your physical strength or moving from place to place?
   b. Do you prefer being in one spot, an office or location for work?

2. Working outside:
   a. Do you prefer being outside for work?
   b. Do you prefer being inside for work?

3. Working remotely:
   a. Do you prefer working from home (or a location of your choice)?
   b. Do you prefer working in a dedicated location or locations?

4. Working within an open setting among others:
   a. Do you prefer to work alongside others and interact with colleagues throughout the day?
   b. Do you prefer to work alone?

5. Equipment:
   a. Do you prefer to work with technical equipment, machinery, or tools?
   b. Do you prefer to work mostly with your knowledge?

6. Communication:
   a. Do you prefer to communicate with coworkers, clients, etc. in person and orally?
   b. Do you prefer to communicate with coworkers, clients, etc. in writing, using collaborative technology, or asynchronously?

7. Geographic location:

    a. Do you want to live in a specific geographic location for work?

    b. Are you open to moving and working anywhere for the right job?

8. Travel:

    a. Do you want to travel as part of your work requirements?

    b. Do you prefer a job that does not require travel?

Look over what you circled as your preferences (if you had any). *Does a pattern emerge? Think through what you did and did not like about your current or past jobs. Did they provide insights into your ideal job context?*

Identify your career needs and motivators

For some people, the intangible environment in which they work is most important based on the feelings they have from the work they are accomplishing. These intangible preferences are based on your personal needs and motivations regarding what you expect from your work. Some individuals are motivated, for example, by achieving challenging or "stretch" goals, whereas others are primarily interested in building close relationships at work. It is important to understand what motivates you because the match between your needs from your career and the work you choose will affect how satisfied and fulfilled you feel doing what you have chosen to do.

UNDERSTAND YOUR MOTIVATIONAL NEEDS

There are some well-researched theories of human motivation that can provide important insights into your ideal career.[8] Most people find satisfaction from some, but possibly not all, of the motivators in the following list. You might have a few main driving motivators, and others to a lesser extent. These motivators are often based on core needs which have been shaped through our earlier lives and are relatively stable across situations, affecting our work preferences and career choices.

As you read through these definitions, think about which one describes you best.

1. **Achievement and recognition**: If you have a high need for achievement, you do not give up easily and will work very hard to achieve your goals. You thrive in competitive situations and will enjoy outperforming your coworkers if it means that you can distinguish yourself (and be promoted). You like to work toward your goals and prefer to succeed on jobs that require the use of your abilities and skills, rather than chance or luck. You do not hesitate to assume additional responsibilities, particularly when they allow you to demonstrate your achievements. A Participation Medal given to everyone for just showing up won't cut it for you.

2. **Social connection and affiliation**: If you have a need for affiliation, you actively participate in social activities and enjoy being liked and considered as an important member in a group. You enjoy working with friends and are motivated by working with others. You tend to accept people readily and try to build friendships and maintain contacts with coworkers. You tend to initiate, participate in, and facilitate social events in the workplace. Team-building activities, corporate retreats, and work-related social events are highly motivational for you. Medieval scribes who spent decades in small rooms writing the Bible by hand wouldn't put this high on their list.

3. **Power**: If you have a need for power, you are highly motivated by opportunities to lead others and have influence. You tend to have a strong desire to take control, influence decisions, and direct the work of other people. You might seek out opportunities for leadership

roles and assume them very naturally. Symbols of power or authority (e.g., job titles and leadership development programs) will generally be highly motivating for you. Your favorite Greek letter is Alpha.

4. **Autonomy**: If you have a need for autonomy, you have a high need for independence and control over your work, how you work, when you work, and where you work. You might seek opportunities to work from home, work independently, be your own boss, or start a company.

5. **Purpose and meaning**: If you have a high need for meaning and purpose, you want to be connected to a higher cause beyond just a paycheck. You might seek out careers where you can help others, where your skills are central for the success of the company, or where you can work directly with a client or customer. Opportunities to have a direct influence on others would be desirable.

6. **Growth and development**: If you have a high need for personal and professional growth you are likely focused on learning and developing new skills. You thrive in environments where you are learning constantly from experiences, from coworkers, and from mentors. You would be motivated to attend a new training program of interest or accept a job assignment where you could stretch and grow your skills. You seek feedback and ask for developmental advice.

While needs are important across all your life's contexts, some people expect their careers (not their personal life) to fulfill certain needs. For example, some people don't have a strong need to build close friendships with their coworkers because their need for affiliation and connection is met by family members and close friends. Other people might find their need for purpose fulfilled from their volunteer work, so they might not need this need to be filled from their career. Consider the following exercise to understand this important distinction in your own life.

	How important is this?	Currently, is this need being met in your personal or professional life?	In the future, do you want this to be met in your personal or professional life?
	1– Not very important 2– Somewhat important 3– Very important	Neither Personal life Professional life Both	Neither Personal life Professional life Both
Achievement and Recognition			
Social Connection and Affiliation			
Power			
Autonomy			
Purpose and Meaning			
Growth and Development			

Do you see a pattern from this exercise? For those motivators you scored "3," you might want to have the needs fulfilled in both your personal and professional lives. For the motivators you scored a "2," you should ensure they are being met in either your personal or professional lives. Anything you scored a "1" wouldn't be much of a motivator.

Compare your current state to your future, ideal career. Are there any needs you need to ensure are fulfilled? Your ideal career might be rooted in the fulfillment of one or more of these.

UNDERSTAND YOUR CAREER ANCHORS

In addition to need fulfillment, another way to think about your career preferences is through the model developed by Dr. Edgar Schein, who found that we each have our own set of *career anchors*, those values or drivers that motivate us to seek and ultimately find satisfaction with our work situations.[9]

You can consider the following list to begin thinking about your career needs and motivators. *Which of the following most closely resonates for you?*

1. **To be a technical or functional expert**: Would you like to be so good at what you do professionally that your expert advice will be sought continually?

2. **To be a leader or manager of people**: Would you like to oversee a business unit, making decisions that affect many people and managing the efforts of others?

3. **To be autonomous or independent**: Would you like to have the freedom to do a job your own way and on your own schedule?

4. **To be secure or stable in your job**: Would you like stable employment and financial security?

5. **To be entrepreneurial or creative/innovative**: Would you like to start and run your own business?

6. **To be dedicated to a cause or to feel that you are serving a greater good**: Would you like to make a real contribution to humanity and society, using your talents in the service of others?

7. **To be competitively challenged**: Would you like a career in which you can solve problems or compete in situations where few can excel or win?

8. **To have work/life balance**: Would you like a career that will permit you to harmonize all important aspects of your life (e.g., your personal life, your family, and your career)?

9. **To have an international career**: Would you like a career that enables you to work in different locations around the world and with people from diverse cultures?[10]

To get a better sense for the context that would be most fulfilling, consider the possible options and identify any of those in which you have a strong preference. *Does any pattern emerge?*

Identify what you don't want

If you have worked through this chapter and still are not sure what you want from your career, it might be easier to identify what you don't want. In this section, let's see if you can gather some insight into your ideal career based on your past work experiences that you *didn't* like.

To begin this assessment, you need only to think about the metaphorical Sunday night, or whatever the last night before your work week starts again. In addition to identifying the way you do (and don't) like to work, the way you feel on Sunday nights could be telling you volumes about your relationship with your current work situation, as we discussed in chapter 1. If you are filled with dread for Monday morning, the source of this dread might need to change to be more fulfilled in your career.

Think through your answers to the following questions to identify what to avoid as you build your career. To help you identify these, answer the following questions:

1. Think about the specific tasks you are dreading this week. List the tasks you dislike the most. Why are they unfulfilling? For example, are the tasks boring, monotonous, thankless, isolated, overwhelming or anxiety-producing? Other reasons might include "This isn't on my job description" or "This is way outside my pay scale" or "Shouldn't my boss be doing this?" or . . . you get the idea.

2. Think about the people with whom you interact. Do you dislike the leader, clients, or colleagues with whom you are working? What is it about them, specifically, that you dislike? For example, are they

disrespectful, distracting, demanding, unprofessional, or rude? Once you've identified them and listed what you dislike, take a deep breath, find that cup of tea or glass of wine, and remember that the goal of the exercise is to find a bright new horizon where you'll never have to think of them again.

3. Think about the climate or culture of your employer. What is it about the context of your work that you dislike? For example, is the company culture too pressured, too disorganized, or too impersonal? Then take another deep breath, another sip, and think about how good it will feel when that job is in your rearview mirror.

4. Think about the resources you need to complete your tasks. What is it about your resources that are lacking in this role? For example, do you not have the skills, equipment, time, or enough help to complete the work? Did your employer last upgrade their tech systems in 2008?

If you have been working for a while, repeat this exercise for previous jobs you have had, even those you had when you were working part-time in school or interning. Go back as far as you can clearly remember. *When looking across your current and past jobs, is a pattern emerging for your definite "dislikes"?*

Please remember, it is normal to dislike some aspects of even the best careers. Paula (and every other professor she knows) dreads the end-of-the course grading. Andy dreads formal conference room meetings and prefers his meetings in cafés or restaurants. Even with an engaging and stimulating career, you might experience some malaise on Sunday evening. It is normal to temporarily mourn the loss of freedom. Remember, even great careers are not great at every moment. Great careers have more of the elements that you find fulfilling, use your talents, and put you in a state of flow. We hope this chapter helped you identify what those are for you.

We know that this chapter has a lot to digest and synthesize. Self-awareness is needed to identify your ideal career but is, admittedly, a process that is challenging for almost everyone. To get the most from the exercises in this chapter, we want you to strive for honesty, accuracy, and an appropriate level of self-confidence.

Some people cannot see their own talents even when others see those talents clearly. On the opposite extreme, some people have a bloated and unwarranted perception of their strengths. Both ends of the continuum are not useful because they can lead you down the wrong career journey. We encourage you to strive for internalized accuracy about your talents and use that knowledge to identify the ideal career.

KEY TAKEAWAYS

- Identify the activities that will put you into a state of flow. Your ideal career should have the greatest number of these activities and the time to accomplish them.

- Identify your natural talents through self-assessments or by asking others who know you well. Leveraging your natural talents will accelerate your career acts toward your ideal career.

- Identify your best work environment. The context for how you work might be equally important (if not more important) than what you do.

- Identify your career needs and motivators. Working with the aspects of work that are the most motivating for you can accelerate your career acts as you move toward your ideal career.

- Identify what you don't want in your ideal career. Ideally, it is best to identify the demotivating aspects of a future career act by avoiding them. Keep in mind that there are no perfect jobs. Even the most fulfilling careers will have tasks and activities that are less engaging.

CHAPTER 3

IDENTIFY YOUR IDEAL CAREER

There is no passion to be found playing small, in settling for a life
that is less than the one you are capable of living.

—NELSON MANDELA

Rana el Kaliouby grew up in Cairo and Kuwait, the daughter of an IT executive and systems anaylst (who was also one of the first female computer programmers in the Middle East).[1] Her home life combined Egyptian/Middle East traditions and elements of Western thinking. Perhaps more unusual, her parents set high standards for their three daughters and put a premium on higher education. This gave Rana the freedom to explore a professional career path. Medicine? Computer science (somewhat "the family business")? Or something else entirely?

With the modern digital age expanding into daily lives all around her, Rana became fascinated with its human ramifications. Specifically, how to humanize technology and bridge the growing gap between humans and machines.

Her amazing life story is told in her memoir, *Girl Decoded*. The book traces her path from "nice Egyptian girl" to world-renowned computer scientist and inventor to successful entrepreneur and CEO (AND mother of two amazing kids and new American citizen).[2] Rana has been powered professionally by passion, curiosity, and the conviction that she could solve a big, intractable problem: the lack of emotional intelligence in computers. "I've been on this mission for over twenty-two years now," says the deputy CEO of Smart Eye and founder and former CEO of her start-up, Affectiva. "For me, this isn't just about human/computer interfaces. It's actually about how we connect with others as human beings and how we connect with one another."

Along the way, she's battled a lot of challenges. She defied cultural norms and made many personal tradeoffs. She immersed herself in the computer science lab at The American University in Cairo, where she advanced, excruciatingly coded and tested, and proved her idea. She entered (and eventually exited) a young marriage to a supportive fellow technology entrepreneur. The marriage included a five-year long-distance relationship (with a child in tow) while she finished her PhD at Cambridge University in the UK on a scholarship ("a dream come true").

There were many ups and downs, as well as incredible moments of serendipity. Most notable among the latter was a chance meeting with Professor Roz Picard from the Massachusetts Institute of Technology (MIT) who was visiting Cambridge, UK, to give a talk. Smitten with Rana's work and her enthusiasm (more on this later), Roz invited her to the US as a postdoc in her group. Eventually the two became co-founders of Affectiva, an MIT spinoff. (Affectiva merged with Smart Eye in 2021.) This event became pivotal in Rana's career.

Another bit of serendipity was "the fastest $5 million ever raised," spawned from a chance meeting in an airport lounge with a former Google executive, investor, and complete stranger. By the end of their dinner at the airport, the executive had contacted several investors, one of whom committed the money. (Not bad for a short trip to Brazil to just give a speech, a trip that she had seriously considered postponing.) What we do for love, indeed.

While Rana's true story may have all the ingredients for a Netflix special, it's the real deal. Regardless of your passion, the lessons she learned are invaluable for those who have an idea and a dream for turning what you love to do into "work": something that you can uniquely do, that others will uniquely value and compensate you for, and that (most importantly) will make you happy.

Rana is most proud of the opportunities she's helped create for others who have joined her on her journey—especially people who joined the Affectiva team early on, many of whom, like her, did not grow up in the US. Playing a small part in their professional, personal, and financial success is something she takes pride in.

Rana offers you some advice for your career, beginning with encouraging you to "find a sense of purpose about what you love. Then make it a cause that other people will care about." This will bring momentum and energy to your career. She also wants you to "have conviction that you can figure it out and solve it." You may not know exactly how to solve something, and it might seem daunting, but your energy and conviction will become contagious. This will let you bring people on board your career journey to help you make it happen. This is vitally important because there's nothing you can do alone. You always need a team: partners, investors, collaborators, storytellers.

It is sometimes tough advice, but Rana suggests that we all need to "be prepared for personal sacrifices or difficult decisions." When she decided to divorce, Rana was still "commuting" between Cairo and Cambridge, Massachusetts, the location of her company's headquarters. She moved to Boston with her two young kids alone, with some stop-gap support from her mother for a few months. But upon her mother's return to Egypt, Rana was literally running the company with two young kids without any support. Not easy.

Rana holds a personal belief that we all should "have faith in ourselves and be prepared to be our own best cheerleader" and has lived this belief. When Rana and her colleagues started the company, she was the chief technology officer. At the urging of the company's early investors, the company hired a seasoned business executive to be the CEO. When he decided to move on, a new CEO was required. Some board members recommended Rana, as the company was "her baby," but she demurred. Her internal narrative told her that she had never been a CEO and thus would fail miserably. (Plot spoiler: she didn't.) The head of sales—who had also never been a CEO, actually—raised his hand and said he'd take it on. And he did, for two years.

On a flight home after delivering a successful TED Talk, Rana started thinking about what a CEO really does, researching and creating a list of all the job responsibilities of a CEO. She realized that she was already doing the job. "So, I mustered all my courage," she says. "Some of my mentors were nudging me to be courageous and basically make the case to become CEO—so I did, with the current CEO, as I did not want to go behind his back."

First, he didn't like the idea. But, fast-forward, they took it to the board for a vote. It was a unanimous vote, and Rana became CEO in May 2016, another pivotal moment for her career and a pivotal moment for the company. "I'm so glad that I overcame my hesitation. It was my biggest obstacle. I had to convince myself first. I see this happen a lot with women on my team," she says.

Rana likes to make room for serendipity, believing that if you're too over-programmed, you'll miss it. "I only met Roz Picard at Cambridge because I had stayed late in my lab that summer to wrap up some things. Normally, I would have been back home with my family," Rana says. "I heard Roz was going to be visiting us in Cambridge and willing to meet. I spent a good two or three weeks prepping for this fifteen-minute meeting. We ended up spending an hour together, and at the end of it, she said, 'Do you want to come work with me as a postdoc?' Of course, that changed the trajectory of my life both personally and professionally, because it started the commute between Boston and Cairo."

She also practices humility, having a willingness to learn from others. She says, "I actually always tell people around me: If they ever feel I've become complacent or stuck-up, they should tell me, because that's a danger sign." She advises career-act-masters to build in humility. Understand that you should always be learning, continuously growing and not stand still—even (or perhaps especially) if you're the boss.

Rana notes that your career journey is not one to take alone and has benefited from having true mentors—and paying it forward by mentoring others. Andy Palmer was the first advisor Affectiva brought on to help with the company. He became a vital mentor to Rana, on everything from operations matters (how to hire a great head of engineering or how to best compensate the sales force) to strategic matters like the next round of funding. When it came to exiting the company, Andy was one of the very first people she reached out to in determining whether to sell the company or raise more money. "Andy has been there for me in every possible way, and I'll never forget that. And I know he doesn't do that with just me, either," she says. "I hope I can be an equally helpful mentor to others as well. It's already usually the best part of my day."

She inspires others to have great career journeys by saying "I like the idea of getting a life, not a job. Find something you're passionate about. Become the world expert in it. And then know that it's going to be tough, so persevere. Own it and own your own voice. It took me many, many years to just embrace who I am, celebrate it and share it with the world. It definitely was not always the case. I've since really enjoyed helping shape the narrative. A lot of people tell me, 'Oh, we had no idea that Egyptian women could do this or do that.' Just breaking stereotypes and amplifying other people's voices has been exciting."

Rana observes that, in the past, the world has tended to pigeonhole people professionally, in buckets. In her case: "You are an entrepreneur." "You are an investor." "You are an influencer." But we are all many things: including, most recently, a podcaster, as Rana and her school-age son learn about non-fungible tokens (NFTs), along with their audience.

Today, the lines in "career" are blurred. "Careers are going to be a portfolio of things that all center around a common cause. We should embrace that, especially young people. I think it's going to be the way of the world," Rana predicts.

We agree whole-heartedly with Rana. Careers today are often like portfolios or mosaics. But, even with multiple career acts and professional identities, we need to start in some direction that motivates us. Journeys with many detours need to start somewhere. Like a great vacation with some amazing, but unexpected, side trips, your career journey might lead you in desirable but unanticipated directions. Your career goal is not set in stone. Each career act can be a new source for insight, opening a new path you hadn't considered. But, like filling the tank with fuel and entering the GPS destination, a career goal starts your career journey.

At this point, we want you to start your career journey with a goal in mind, any direction for that first step. Everyone's career goal will be different in content and precision. For some people, having a single, clear professional identity (e.g., doctor, baker, rabbi, massage therapist, geneticist) is their ideal career. For others, their ideal career will be more of an idea of what they want to accomplish or solve (e.g., improve the lives of children in need, have the best bakery in town, use technology to network artists).

In the previous chapter, we offered a series of exercises to identify what places you into a state of flow, your natural talents, your best work environment, your career needs, motivators, and what you don't want in your career. We gave you a metaphorical jigsaw puzzle. You flipped over the pieces and found the corners. Best of all, you were able to see that you have all the pieces you need (nothing's worse than finishing a jigsaw puzzle and finding you're one piece short.) Now, let's see if the image can emerge in this chapter. We have different approaches for you to achieve this goal:

- Your professional identity
- Your greater purpose or big idea
- Your career dreams and their insights into your ideal career

Each of these approaches might point you to the same goal. Then again, they might suggest very different careers, signaling that you probably need more information about your options. Both are reasonable outcomes. Take the time to set a clear first goal but remember you are not taking an oath to achieve it. This isn't a commitment; it is a way to start your important journey. You'll be able to enter a stronger destination into your job GPS than "I'll take any job that's better than what I'm doing now."

Before we start, we need to remind you that your career goal is yours and yours alone. It is not the one your parent or partner wants for you. It is not the one your mentor or manager thinks you should have. You'll need to be self-focused (or even selfish) for this one chapter. We promise that we will bring back others' needs and your family responsibilities in later chapters. For now, you are just thinking about you.

The reason your career goal needs to be a personal decision is that it is based on what you and you alone find intrinsically rewarding. If you have ever spent time finishing a Sunday crossword puzzle, weeding your vegetable garden, or running a marathon, then you know that achieving a self-set goal is highly rewarding for its own sake. These intrinsic rewards (e.g., the solved puzzle or a weed-free garden) are motivating because they result from the goal you set for yourself based on what you enjoy, a sense of personal growth, an interest, or a personal challenge.

Intrinsic rewards are different from extrinsic rewards, the rewards received from completing a goal that others have set for you, such as incentives or compensation. Research has found that the more you enjoy your work, the more engaged you will be, but the more you focus on the compensation of your work, the less engaged you will be.[3] Just ask anyone who has had the job of weeding someone else's garden for money. It just isn't the same (unless, of course, they love to pull weeds, in which case they've found their calling). Your ideal career should be an intrinsically rewarding goal you set for yourself based on your sense of purpose, passion, or interest.

Identifying a career goal based on what you—*and you alone*—find intrinsically rewarding is challenging. You have spent [fill in your age here] years being *extrinsically* rewarded for being "good" (a good student, a good son/daughter, a good employee, etc.). This socialization by your parents, family, education, generation, nation, and the like, has shaped how you behave, how you expect others to behave, and the way you make decisions—including your career decisions. This is especially true if you were socialized in tighter or more collectivist cultures, ones in which family expectations had a greater control over your choices as a child.[4] In looser or more individualist cultures, people had more independence to pursue the careers they wanted.

Whether you are from a tight or loose culture, the way you were socialized will affect how you think about career choices. To illustrate, respond to this question without overthinking: *How do you judge a teenager who quits school to follow a dream to become a singer or actor? Reckless and impetuous or courageous and talented?* Be honest. The way you judge this teenager is based on your underlying values which form your subjective perceptions (e.g., what is right or wrong, what is good or bad, what is successful or unsuccessful). In this case, the value you place on education as either "important" or "unimportant". Incidentally, many stars including Rihanna, Marlon Brando, Whoopi Goldberg, and Al Pacino did not have a traditional high school graduation experience.[5]

How you were culturally socialized is not a conspiracy, forcing you to make unfulfilling career choices. Cultural socialization is a normal part of being human, the social oxygen you have been breathing since you were born. It works like this: our primitive brain seeks approval and keeps us behaving in ways that are reinforced. Behaving as expected by those in our life (e.g., family, school, community) will keep us in "good graces," connected to, and accepted by the other members of our tribe, so to speak. Our primitive brain knows that some level of conformity will keep us safe because we are accepted by our group.

While normal, we might need to acknowledge the potentially powerful effect that cultural socialization has had on us and our career choices. We want to ensure that we are not selecting an extrinsically driven career, one that would make our tribe proud. Rather, we want you to find a career goal that will be intrinsically motivating to you.

Identify your professional identity

Do you have a career goal based on the **identity** ascribed to an occupation or profession? A professional identity will make you feel a certain way to say, "this is my career" (e.g., proud to be a librarian, tech CEO, or rock star). It will give you the perception of your position within your group (e.g., everyone appreciates the town librarian, admires that tech CEO, or wants the rock star's autograph). It will give you a sense of belonging to that profession (e.g., a member of the American Library Association, Technology CEO Council, Rock and Roll Hall of Fame). This is known as choosing to DO something so you can BE known for something, or as the unintentional career expert Frank Sinatra once put it, DO-BE DO-BE-DO.

If you have a career goal in mind, fill that career goal in the blank for each of the following sentences. Then, go back and reread the sentences with your career goal filled in. Pause on each sentence and ask yourself "is this true?" If you can honestly say "yes," your career goal likely has a professional identity that is meaningful for you—and you know the direction your career journey will likely take.

1. I respect people who are a [name of career goal].

2. I would feel a sense of personal pride to be able to say I am a [name of career goal].

3. I will work hard to become a [name of career goal].

4. I know what it takes to become a [name of career goal].

5. I am intrinsically motivated to become a [name of career goal].

Your professional identity might be associated with a defined *occupation* (e.g., dentist, accountant, journalist, landscaper, coder, bartender) or it might be based on the identity connected to an *interest or passion*. Let's consider both.

AN OCCUPATION

Occupations are a series of related jobs within job families that share a set of knowledge, skills, and abilities. Doctors, plumbers, actors, and teachers are examples of occupational groups. Within a given occupation, skills are generally transferable across a variety of work situations. If your ideal career goal is an occupation, chances are high that the journey to achieve your career goal will follow easily identifiable career acts. Physicians, for example, go to medical school and many become medical residents after completing their degree. Research academics like Paula complete a PhD and get a university tenure-track job, and eventually become associate professors with tenure and then full professors.

If you are interested in exploring an occupation as a career goal, engage in the following activities:

- Speak to individuals who are currently in the occupation you believe would be your ideal career. People, for the most part, enjoy talking about their career journeys. Always speak to more than one person. Keep speaking to people in that occupation until you start to hear overlapping stories and a clear picture is painted of the occupation— both good and bad. The bonus of this exercise: you will broaden your network of people in this occupation. Avoid family members and friends, they are already in your network and might be using what they know about you to shift their story. Have a structured set of questions about their career path; the knowledge, skills, and abilities needed for the career act; and their thoughts on how the career might be changing in the future. Here are some questions you can ask those with your ideal career:

- How did you attain your current career? Is your path typical or atypical for those in your career?

- What experiences or education prepared you for this role? What experiences or education do you wish you had that would have made your career even more successful?

- Do you know others in your same role? If so, how did they become successful in this career role?

- What are some things most people do not realize about this career?

- If I wanted to do exactly what you are doing, what steps would I need to take? What are the factors impeding success at each step? What are the factors facilitating success at each step?

- Observe. If you can, we also recommend observing those individuals who are currently engaged in your ideal career. Shadow someone on a typical workday. Again, we suggest you not choose a close friend or a family member because they, although well-intentioned, might offer the type of evaluative information you should be concluding on your own. Try to shadow multiple people and the same person on multiple days—because the same career acts might change depending on who is in the role and the day you are observing. Be sure to let them know beforehand when you'll be shadowing them, so they don't report you to security.

- Visit industry websites to learn more about selected occupations. For example, when Paula meets someone who is interested in her field of organizational psychology, she will generally offer her explanation of the field but then send them to the Society for Industrial and Organizational Psychology website[6] to learn about the profession. Many outstanding websites associated with industry groups are available to provide information on the knowledge, skills, and abilities needed for any given career. You can also access job posting boards on various websites to better understand the type of knowledge, skills, abilities, education, and experiences that employers seek.

- Learn about individuals' career journeys. Autobiographies, biographies, and some documentaries about individuals are great ways to learn how (usually famous) people achieved what they did. You can learn from them and their stories. You can be motivated by them. You can even follow in their footsteps, to some extent. Remember though, everyone's journey will be unique.

- Join professional networking groups on LinkedIn, which virtually convene like-minded people interested in certain professions. Read about their professional challenges and successes, what they are writing about and discussing. Their posts, articles, and comments will give you a sense of what the occupation entails.

- Explore O*NET. Described in the previous chapter, O*NET is a great source of information about occupations. You can look up almost any occupation and learn about the tasks performed on the job, required areas of knowledge, skills, and abilities to perform the job, and the context of the work.

AN INTEREST OR PASSION

Your professional identity might be associated with an interest or passion. As illustrated in Rana's career at the start of this chapter, having an interest or passion can be one of the most enjoyable ways to persevere through your career journey. The world is full of people who have taken their passions, interests, or even hobbies, originally enjoyed solely for personal pleasure, and turned them into thriving careers.

The possible ways to turn an interest or passion with tangible outcomes (e.g., art, sewing, baking, cooking, photography, playing a musical instrument) into a career might be clear (e.g., artist, tailor, chef, photographer, musician) but not necessarily easy. Before you turn your passion or interest into a career goal, consider the following three (often overlooked) issues:

Understand the psychological shift: You are now working for clients, not engaging in a hobby for yourself. You might lose freedoms enjoyed as a hobbyist when you begin to have customers or clients. Paula's sister Terry quilts wonderfully and periodically talks about making this a profitable hobby (usually when Paula brings it up). When pressed on why she doesn't, she says that quilting is her "release," her way to unwind at the end of the day and she does not want to lose this by placing client demands on the way she sews. This is insightful and highly relevant for those who view their hobby as a personal outlet and would not want to fill orders to customer specifications. Alternatively, you can take a different approach and create what you like, hoping you'll find clients or customers who will appreciate and purchase what you want to sell. In this case, the trade-off is the preservation of personal freedom enjoyed as a hobbyist for a potential limitation on your range of clients or customers. Your call—just think it through.

Know how to value your time along with the tangible costs to price your goods or services: Even if you only want to engage in your profitable hobby for a few hours each week, value your time as if you were doing this full-time. Try this: Ask yourself: What income would I (realistically) want to be making if this were my sole source of income? Divide this out to an hourly wage and multiply by the hours you spend on one unit of your profitable hobby. Add in overhead. Add in material costs. Add in taxes. Decide what profit you would like to make (considering your level of skill, experience, etc.). Too many people undervalue their time and their other intangible assets (such as their skill level).

Know your competition: Hobbyists can operate in a delightful bubble; they can be blissfully unaware of the cost, quality, or marketability of whatever they produce. If you want to make melted-bottle spoon rests for yourself, family, and friends, do you really care about competition? No. When you begin to market your hobby as a source for potential income generation, be sure you understand the competition and the potential market, the demand for your goods and services.

Identify your greater purpose or big idea

When you identify your ideal career goal based on your sense of purpose, you will be more motivated to expend personal resources to achieve the goal. Unfortunately, for many, having "a sense of purpose" means something metaphysical, a divine sense of what you were placed on the planet to accomplish. That divine intervention is a spiritual calling and is quite valid for the many religious leaders who have had them.

When we talk about identifying *your* purpose, we are not talking about spiritual callings; rather, we are talking about your idea of what you want to use your talents to accomplish. Your purpose will be a sense, a feeling, or a gut instinct that there is some problem you'd like to solve or a big idea you have. Your purpose or big idea will be inspired by the world around you and your life experiences.

To identify your purpose or big idea, ask yourself the following three questions:

- *What in the world gives you a strong emotional reaction, whether anger or joy?* Reflect on whether there is something in those emotional experiences pointing you to your purpose or big idea. Many entrepreneurs started their businesses with a big idea born from a problem they wanted to solve. Travis Kalanick and Garrett Camp, co-founders of Uber, claimed to have started the global ride-sharing application because they couldn't get a cab on a winter evening in Paris.[7] Sara Blakely, the founder of Spanx, began the shapewear company because she was frustrated that she had a pair of pants in her closet that she could not wear because she did not have the correct undergarment.[8]

- *What gives you a deep sense of frustration that "you could do that better"?* If you can harness your frustration into a career goal, you might have the extra acceleration to make it a reality. John and Patrick Collison, co-founders of Stripe, started this company to accept online payments, frustrated that all the systems available at the time when they were building start-ups were too difficult to set up.[9]

- *What problem do you believe is the most important for the world to solve today?* Reid Hoffman, the co-founder of LinkedIn, said that he started LinkedIn because he wanted to "try to help humanity evolve" by fostering connections across people. Less focused on whether to be an entrepreneur or an employee, he wanted to follow his purpose. His story is an inspirational one for how to think about your own career. Both of us are fans of Reid Hoffman's book *The Start-Up of You: Adapt to the Future, Invest in Yourself, and Transform Your Career*. In this book, Hoffman describes an approach to identify a career goal by thinking of what people need today—what would help them solve their problems. In doing so, you know your career goal will add value and be in demand.

As the founder of Koa Labs, Andy has seen many would-be entrepreneurs over the years. Those who stand out above others have a deep sense of purpose, are motivated by that purpose, and are visibly driven by their big idea. To make decisions on whether to back a start-up, Andy looks for the founder's personal motivation, their big idea, and their skills to create a business from these.

IF YOU NEED SOME MOTIVATION TO DREAM . . .

What did you want to be as a child? If you feel silly answering this question, please watch Randy Pausch's YouTube video called "The Last Lecture."

On September 18, 2007, Professor Randy Pausch of Carnegie Mellon University gave a lecture, a lecture that would be eventually heard by millions but written for his three young children. Randy's lecture motivated us to dream again and inspired us to stay true to those dreams. The lecture and the book, titled *The Last Lecture*, touched millions of hearts around the world because he spoke of how he had lived his childhood dreams, encouraging us all to keep our own childhood dreams alive and make them come true. He spoke with urgency to a world desperate to dream again. He spoke with authority as someone who had successfully lived his childhood dreams. He spoke with credibility about life because, at forty-seven, he was, in fact, near death. Ten months after delivering this lecture, Randy died from pancreatic cancer. Randy's illness gave the world a gift, the license to dream and not apologize for wanting to fulfill those dreams.

Your career dreams and their insights

Many people lose their ability to dream about an ideal career somewhere in their late teens or early twenties, the time when the dominant message is that we should "get serious about our future." This advice throws water on the fire of young adult passions, forcing them to concede that they are unlikely to become supermodels, professional football players, ballerinas, or rock stars. As we noted at the start of this chapter, this career goal concession could be a function of social pressure to "get real." Then again, it could be rooted in a heightened self-awareness of our personal limits: We discover that out there exist people who are more beautiful, more athletic, better dancers, and better guitarists. We start to see our realities and, perhaps (for the first time), the limits of our own skills and abilities.

But there is a wide-open space between an "unattainable fantasy career" and a "get serious career" that allows plenty of room for creativity to fulfill the underlying motivators of why the fantasy was attractive. In other words, we need to root our ideal career goal in the reality of our talents without losing sight of why it was motivating.

To think this through a bit more, start with a dream or fantasy career and ask yourself the following three questions:

The first question is: *what would your ideal career be if you could do whatever you wanted—anything at all—without fear of failure or being limited by your natural talents*? If you are having a difficult time answering this, return to the exercises in the previous chapter and have the conversation with some close friends or loved ones. Those we love can often be more creative with our talents than we can for ourselves. (The bonus is that it makes for a fun cocktail or coffee conversation.) If you're thinking of a career in finance but they suggest occupations like personal chef or gourmet chocolatier, be prepared to ask: "Is this going to benefit you or me?"

The second question is: *why is this career so appealing*? Be honest. There is no one here to judge you. (You might want to leave the friends out of this part of the exercise.) Try to identify all the underlying reasons for wanting this dream career.

The third question is: *what are the plausible alternative careers that would satisfy the same motivators*? To answer this question, you need to be creative. If you are falling short on ideas bring those friends back for another coffee or cocktail and ask them: *"What careers result in . . .?"* You can ask the same question to career counselors or even spend some time with a solid Google search. At this point, you are just brainstorming alternatives. After you finish brainstorming, do any seem appealing? If so, you might have found your ideal career goal.

For example, if you dreamed of being a *race car driver* because you *love speed*, an alternative career might be *airline pilot*. If you *love the adrenaline rush*, an alternative career might be *firefighter*. If you *love cars*, an alternative career might be an *automotive engineer*. Andy, like many former college athletes, had success after college playing the sport (rugby) but did not become a professional athlete. In his case, he loved the intensity of playing a competitive rugby match and the camaraderie of the team. The outlet he found to satisfy both, while going easier on his body, was entrepreneurship and investing in founders to help them follow their passions. While not playing professional rugby, he built a career around what made that career attractive.

WHAT IF YOU STILL HAVE NO IDEA FOR WHAT YOUR IDEAL CAREER GOAL MIGHT BE?

If you are still unsure of a possible career goal, it might mean that you need to spend more time with the previous chapter to build self-awareness. Return to that chapter to identify what puts you into a state of flow, your talents, your ideal work environment, career motivators, and what you know you don't want in your career.

If you need a more active approach to take a first step, remember that you can do the following:

- Gather some work experiences. Try taking a part-time job, entry-level job, or internship in an industry of interest. You will learn more about what careers you like and dislike within an industry which seems attractive.

- Volunteer. Volunteer work will often help you better understand how you like to work.

- Seek advice from a career counselor. If you are past your school days when counselors and advisors are part of the educational system, you might need to hire an independent career counselor. There are many professionals who offer excellent career advice for a fee. If you need assistance finding someone, we can help.

Reality check

Reread your notes from the previous chapter and add the insights from this one. Are you now able to identify an ideal career goal based on your career needs, motivators, and how you like to work? As with all great careers, you need to make decisions while being honest with yourself and gathering data about yourself, what you enjoy, what makes you happy, what really interests you, and what motivates you.

Once you have identified your career goal, we want you to do a quick reality check before starting the journey:

- **What natural attributes does your ideal career require, if any?** Some careers are bound by natural ability or attributes, whereas most can be achieved as a function of raw motivation, effort, practice, and commitment. As an example, if your career goal is to be a military fighter pilot, you will need to have normal color vision and vision that is correctable to 20/20. Vision, as an example, is a natural attribute. A severe allergy to dogs might challenge your dream of becoming a world-renowned poodle groomer.

- **Do you have the strength of character to overcome doubters and naysayers?** It was Henry Ford who famously said, "Whether you think you can, or think you can't—you're right." The self-fulfilling prophecy is real when you are told that your ideal career is unrealistic, especially when the words are uttered by someone you love and trust. Some family and friends will be in your life without knowing the details of your career goals. Instead of wasting the energy to combat their concerns and doubts, build your self-efficacy along with your skills for success and surround yourself with people who will support you through your career journey. Kindly Aunt Gladys who always said you'd never amount to anything? Keep your conversations with her about the weather.

- **Are you realistic about what it will take to achieve your career goal?** Some of the most glamorous careers involve periods of tremendous boredom or tasks that are the opposite of glamorous. Be certain to have a clear picture of what the career journey will likely entail.

We hope that this and the previous chapter have given you the insight needed to identify an ideal career. Remember that this is not carved in stone. You have fueled the tank and the destination is in your GPS. That said, you have control over changing the destination along with the route to get there. The ideal career you identify today could change in the future as your self-awareness builds, your network grows, opportunities open, and circumstances transform your priorities.

KEY TAKEAWAYS

- Have a career goal and some sense of what it will take to achieve that goal.

- Identify the role of cultural programming in your choice of a career goal. Be sure it is what you really want and not what others want for you.

- Identify a career goal that connects with your greater purpose or big idea.

- If you are having a difficult time identifying a career goal, analyze your idea of a dream career for insight into why you want a certain career.

- Recognize whether you are attracted to a professional identity. This might be a specific occupation or a profession that is born from an interest or passion.

SOCIAL MEDIA CHALLENGES

These challenges are meant to showcase your dedication to your career journey and offer appreciation to those who have helped you along the way. In addition, these challenges are a way for you to publicly commit to a goal. Research has found that you are far more likely to achieve your goal when you make a public declaration of the goal. Post these to Instagram, Facebook, LinkedIn, or whatever social media platform you use. When you post, please tag #LiveforaLiving and the hashtag for the challenge.

1. #MyCareerVisionBoard

Create a digital or physical vision board that represents your ideal career. Use images, words, and symbols—anything that is a visual representation of your career aspiration. Share it on social media if you want to declare your goal. You might inspire others to do the same.

2. #MyCareerProgress

Create a series of posts or videos showcasing the steps you are taking to build your ideal career. Each post can represent a step you are taking, and over time, chronicle your progress. Include the experiences, certificates, achievements, new skills, and insights. You might use this challenge to publicly thank those who helped you through each step.

3. #MyIdealCareer

Share a visual, such as a photo or an image, representing you in your ideal career. Describe how this career would align with your other life priorities.

4. #InspirationPlaylist

Create an inspirational playlist of songs that motivate you to achieve your goals. Share the list with your network and encourage others to add their favorite songs to the list.

5. #BestWorkspace

Share a photo of your best workspace. This should be the place where you can get into a state of flow, whether in a coffee shop, in your office, or at home. Describe how this workspace supports your creativity and focus.

PART 2

PLAN YOUR JOURNEY

CHAPTER 4

CRAFT YOUR CAREER
ACTS OVER TIME

We make a living by what we get, but we make a life by what we give.
—WINSTON CHURCHILL

"I've always wanted to do outlandish and significant things, primarily things that would help ordinary people do extraordinary things," says veteran CEO, founder, and entrepreneur Frank Moss.[1] As a kid growing up in 1950s to 1960s Baltimore, he was a self-described nerd (but a "multi-faceted nerd"). He was interested in everything from space, medicine, and astrophysics to biology and art.

Basically, he wanted to live in the future. For starters, Frank aspired to work in the US Space Program, the National Aeronautics and Space Administration (NASA). He went on to spend decades crafting a series of career acts to meet his goal—with a lot of help from serendipity, successes, failures, "just raising my hand," and conversations with many, many people.

As a Princeton undergraduate and MIT graduate student, Frank studied aeronautical engineering, which involved using early computers in designing guidance and control systems for spacecraft. Then the NASA Space Program shut down unceremoniously in the early 1970s after the Apollo 17 mission. "We put a man on the moon, and nobody cared," Frank rues. This shift in NASA priorities marked a tightening of the abundant career opportunities for aeronautical engineers like Frank. He needed a new career act.

Frank's next career act was a leap of faith mixed with some serendipity. Although not a computer scientist and with very few programming skills under his belt, Frank came to the attention of IBM, which was just starting to think about networked/distributed computer networks. Frank's PhD thesis was on the topic of applying guidance and control for routing systems for the ARPANET, a precursor to the Internet. Frank working for IBM in the 1970s was a career match made in heaven.

Hired as a researcher at IBM's famed Yorktown Heights Research Lab, Frank quickly became one of IBM's youngest directors and responsible for evangelizing and advancing networked and distributed computing at the mainframe company. His prospects for an executive career at IBM were bright. When he decided to leave IBM to pursue his growing interest in personal computing technology (where a wave of new start-ups was springing up and leading, including Apollo, Stellar, and Lotus), his employer was shocked: leaving IBM Just. Wasn't. Done. Ever.

What followed was a series of technology-evangelist, product-leader, and executive positions with companies promoting the redistribution of enterprise computing power. This culminated in Frank being named CEO of start-up Tivoli Systems in Austin, Texas, which went public in March 1995 and a year later reversed-merged with (you guessed it) IBM. In 1998, he retired from IBM as Chairman of Tivoli, returned with his family to New England (a life goal), and co-founded the first of several more enterprise tech start-ups accelerating the power-shift happening in computing: from institutions to individuals.

But there was something missing. This was brought home to Frank on his fiftieth birthday. His adult son reminded him: "You always told us to do meaningful things for the world. So why are you still selling business software to guys in suits?" It was time for Frank to flip his experience.

Frank in fact had been thinking about his "outlandish" mission: empowering ordinary people to do extraordinary things. Tivoli and his tech start-ups had empowered ordinary businesspeople by using information technology. How might this help in other, perhaps more important, areas?

He'd been reading extensively about the challenges facing health care, specifically in accelerating the availability of new medicines for patients. Building on his now-extensive experience in information technology, he leveraged his expertise into powerful, satisfying experiences in a completely new industry: biomedical engineering and drug discovery.

Enter Frank's career act number three. Using his reputation and (by now) extensive connections, he wrangled introductions. He talked to a lot of people in the industry, even when many conversations didn't come to much. This introduced him to a whole new community of world-renowned experts in biotechnology and new opportunities, given his lifelong habit of raising his hand and volunteering to help out on projects. He eventually was invited to chair a committee formed to advise Harvard Medical School on forming a Department of Systems Biology that would apply digital technology to biology—the school's first new department in a hundred years. (It did.)

In 2001, at age fifty-four, he co-founded his first biotechnology start-up, Infinity Pharmaceuticals. At Infinity, Frank flipped the script on his career to unlock a new, more gratifying mission and in the process inspired several leading computer scientists, software engineers, and entrepreneurs to follow him into the life sciences—pursuing missions to help doctors and researchers discover important new medicines that make a difference in people's lives. The Infinity team felt immense pride when it treated the first cancer patient. Frank started advising other start-ups in this new field.

Frank was ready for his fourth career act when a once-in-a-lifetime opportunity cropped up: to head the famous MIT Media Lab, which shared his mission of empowering individuals through digital technologies. On the surface, this opportunity may have seemed like a distraction, but it was completely consistent with his passions, interests, and talents (including his ability to express himself creatively). He created a special practice in disruptive, digital technology–empowered health care and trained/advised students as a professor, several of whom went on to create their own high-profile start-ups (one that he co-founded and went on to be acquired by a large health-technology company).

Today, in his early seventies and now in the "giving-back career act," Frank continues to advise mission-driven start-ups and organizations at the intersection of IT and medicine. A main activity today is ArtLifting, a nonprofit that uses the arts and digital technology to improve the human condition. His advice for others at all stages of their career acts: "Have lots of conversations. Most may not amount to anything but, with the right focus, they'll put you in the right place where opportunity—and serendipity—will find you. And that's the name of the game."

Frank's career was not perfect. It was not linear or predictable. He did, however, remain true to his passions, interests, and talents and enjoyed ful-fillment throughout the journey. His career engagement continues as he mentors and advises others. In our experience, like Frank, the most fulfilled people never stop working. Instead, they view work as an integral and satis-fying part of life, embracing (either consciously or unconsciously) career acts throughout life.

Like Frank, those who are most fulfilled in their careers turn the retire-ment logic inside out with fulfilling career acts that grow over time. They neither stop working in retirement nor do they wait for retirement to expe-rience fulfillment. Throughout their careers, they remain committed to stimulating income-generating activities that build on each other so they can reap the rewards (and share them) in their later years. They steadily and stra-tegically invest in acquiring career acts that make them a valued and engaged contributor to the world at every age. They are not afraid to take a risk or make a change. They know that the earlier they start, the more successful and fulfilled they will be.

We want you to consider your career acts as purposeful investments you make in yourself, like a Roth Individual Retirement Account (IRA) to achieve your ideal career. By steadily and strategically investing in yourself, you create an asset that gives you freedom throughout your career journey and a career that pays off later in life with "tax-free" career and life satisfaction. As with a Roth IRA, the earlier you start to invest and the smarter you are about your decisions, the better off you will be.

Remember that nothing is carved in stone. You may add career acts along the way as you move toward a single ideal career you identified in the previous chapter. You might change course completely. Unlike an IRA, there's no substantial penalty for early career withdrawal, especially when you find another career to invest yourself in. We want you to remain open to the possibility that the ideal career you identify today could change in the future as your self-awareness builds, your network grows, and circumstances change.

Research has found that those who are most successful in directing the course of their careers have taken the steps to learn new skills, network, and be financially prepared for each successive phase. Maintaining this combination of planning and open-minded exploration offers the best chance for achieving your ideal career. This approach will also provide you with a diversity of interesting career acts that might even pleasantly surprise you. We want you to enjoy the best of this career journey, with all its exciting twists!

To think about your career in phases, we suggest you consider your career an asset that builds over time, like that Roth IRA. In this chapter, we offer *five phases of ideal careers*, each one with its own goals and mindsets. Each phase has associated career acts that are hallmarks of success in that phase:

1. **Starter Phase:** Career acts in this phase are opportunities for exploration and self-discovery. They include first jobs, part-time (sometimes minimum wage) jobs, and internships. They also include investments in your knowledge and skills, such as college, certificate programs, and apprenticeship or training programs. Some people use this phase to sample careers as if they were trying dishes from a tasting menu without having to worry about wine pairs.

2. **Foundational Phase**: Career acts in this phase are your initial full-time opportunities that are directly related to your ideal career. Usually this is the time to focus on building a strong foundation through one solid career act, but, at this stage, you might also have an additional career act, such as a freelance opportunity that leverages skills or interests you have.

3. **High-Growth Phase**: The career acts in this phase are the roles you select to reflect both your professional identity and how others see you within your profession, industry, or field. This is the phase in which you start to have options based on your marketable skills and your growing professional reputation. In this stage, you might even have the skills and resources to grow an entrepreneurial venture or add an additional income-generating activity. You're being asked to connect on LinkedIn by dozens of people you don't know.

4. **High-Focus Phase**: The career acts in this phase are as close as most come to achieving their ideal career or having every piece of their ideal career portfolio. At this stage, you have a professional niche, a great reputation, and are sought out for your unique skills. If you have an entrepreneurial venture or additional income-generating activities, others are likely working for you, with your work values reflected in the organization you have created.

5. **Give-Back Phase**: In this phase, career acts are the opportunities to impart what you have learned to others and share your success. At this stage you are actively involved in mentoring, teaching, and coaching so others can achieve. With greater financial success, you might become an angel investor or a philanthropist to accelerate others through their career journeys. Most find this the most satisfying phase of their career journey. Time to head out to your vacation home and write your memoir.

For most people, ideal careers happen in these five phases over the course of their career journey. While these phases hold for many, we recognize that not everyone will go through each of these five phases nor spend the same amount of time in each phase. To illustrate, here are some exceptions:

- While rarely as fast as the outside world thinks, those who are thought of as *overnight successes* achieve their career goals at a faster rate than most, possibly skipping phases along the way. These people—generally prodigies, visionaries, or those who are exceedingly lucky—achieve the height of their careers early in their lives. Andy sees this with young entrepreneurs who have a great invention or innovation and the skills to grow a company early in their careers. They often go on to start or help build multiple companies throughout their careers.

- *Non-careerists* will find a job that seems comfortable enough, usually within the first few phases, and decide to hold there. They might dedicate more time to nonwork or volunteer endeavors unrelated to their professional income-earning path.

- *Career changers* also take a nonlinear path. They move part of the way through these early phases and then, with the benefit of insight and self-awareness, change their career goals completely. We see this most typically when students change their majors or when mid-career professionals work in a field only to realize this is not really what they want. They change to something different, such as starting a business or returning to school for a different degree.

- *Serial careerists* achieve much in their careers, but before entering the final phases, they start another (very different) career that requires them to return to starter and foundational phases. Paula sees examples of this at the university when corporate executives return to the university to pursue PhDs. These executives are close to the give-back phase of their corporate job but opt to use their talents to become research-oriented, tenure-track university professors—very different from the corporate path on which they were already succeeding.

There is another deviation from the sequential career phases: *simultaneous career acts*. Simultaneous career acts are multiple parallel career goals. They follow the phases described in this chapter, but are on multiple paths concurrently, each in a different phase. When people have the greatest control over their careers, they often engage in simultaneous career acts (described more in the next chapter). These multiple concurrent career acts are foundational for creating a portfolio career, an approach we enthusiastically support.

Whatever works best for you, whether linear or simultaneous career acts, our goal for this chapter is to give you a way to think about career progression from the perspective of choices, goals, skills, and mindsets at the various phases. As always, we offer considerations, not prescriptions, to maximize your career acts associated with each phase.

Phase 1: Starter career acts

If you are a person who is starting to think about a career but who has not yet started to work, you might be in your teens or entering the workforce for the first time after raising a family or being a caregiver. Whatever the age, you need to start your career journey somewhere. To that end, we encourage you to begin the journey with a starter career act that moves you toward an ideal career goal.

We recognize (and respect) that you might not yet have an ideal career in mind. Regardless, the starter career act phase is a nice time to form your relationship with work and to start to understand how you do (and don't) like to work (see chapter 2). If you try a starter act and it's not a career you want to make a long-term commitment to, you can leave without any awkward "it's not you, it's me" conversations. You might even have the ideal career goal in mind (see chapter 3) and are ready to start the journey.

SELECTING STARTER CAREER ACTS

We want this starter career acts phase to be a period of enjoyable exploration. Realistically, some of what you will be doing for starter career acts, frankly, will be boring, frustrating, and likely underpaid. Even so, you should be gaining self-awareness, identifying the work experiences you like and dislike. More subtly, you will learn how you work best and maybe start to identify your natural talents. This is the shallow end of the career pool.

In this phase, you should be insatiably gathering data about yourself. Every experience is valuable in this phase, provided you take the time to reflect on what it taught you about your likes, dislikes, natural talents, and the like. If you are past this stage of your career journey, don't skip over this section. Instead, use it to reflect on your earliest experiences, remembering what you appreciated, valued, and enjoyed from your starter career acts— and what you did not.

First jobs as starter career acts. If you are like most, your first job might be something part-time, requiring few skills, and lacking lucrative compensation. These starter career acts are fountains of knowledge however, if you are willing to reflect on them.

Paula remembers one of her first jobs as a teenager working in a tuxedo rental shop, a job that required not much skill or training, that had her working with two of her closest friends from high school and earning the job title of "certified formalwear consultant" by age seventeen. She describes:

My career in formalwear was admittedly short-lived but I learned: (1) I like to be busy (wedding and prom seasons were insane, but fun). (2) I enjoy a sense of belonging to the team—the parties were amazing. (3) I like to be in an elite environment (tuxedo rentals seemed posh compared to those of my burger-flipping classmates), and (4) I like to work with people I call friends. I also learned that vacuuming was one of the housekeeping tasks that wasn't all that bad because it gave me a sense of visual accomplishment. In retrospect, I always ended up vacuuming because one of my best friends (and back then, coworker) Beth was better at everything related to the cash register. To this day, finances are not my strength. Forty years later, I bought a Roomba.

Andy's first job was working for a small computer reseller, Valcom, in Portland, Maine. As a junior in college, he helped them with marketing. His boss, Michael Donovan, was a fantastic leader who taught Andy many things; one of his favorite lessons was that no matter what task they were doing, it was important to be detail-oriented and fact-check every piece of work. Andy also learned from Michael that no matter how much time they had put into something, it could always be better. Andy recalls, "No matter what I was doing for Michael, he always found opportunities to improve my work and instilled in me a strong belief in continuous improvement. No matter how proud I was of a piece of work—a marketing brochure, a database of customers and prospects, some code for a customer—that it could always improve if I had more time, energy, and attention."

For both of us, there was an unlikely energetic rush in renting tuxedos and selling computers. Realizing the joy of compensation and the sense of accomplishment and belonging from those first jobs set an important foundation for our relationship with work. Starter career acts are often as enlightening as they are underpaid. Don't expect your first work experience to be perfect or long lasting. If you take what you can from them, they will provide great opportunities to explore your interests, learn which features of work you like (and don't like), and explore how your talents could be valuable to the world.

As you start this journey, all experiences are good. Paula learned about customer service at the tuxedo rental shop, honed after a few too many wrong color bow-ties. Andy will never forget the importance of attention to detail and continuous improvement in work.

Beyond learning about a potential field of interest, you might learn about how to deal with customers and the public, how to collaborate with coworkers, and how to recover from mistakes or failures. You'll see how an organization works. These lessons—each one valuable—are best learned in practice, instead of the classroom.

Internship programs as starter career acts. If you are itching to get a jump-start on your professional career acts (and have the luxury to skip over the minimum wage job), there are many programs today that link new entrants to the workforce with experiential opportunities in organizations, whether paid or unpaid. These programs can help you accumulate career experience and road-test careers even before college. Check your local community organizations and high schools for these programs and don't assume that you do not have the means to find one of these programs. For example, there are a growing number of innovative nonprofit programs that are leveling the career playing field for ambitious youth and young adults who may have fewer opportunities due to their family's socioeconomic circumstances.

In our area (Boston/Cambridge), there's Beacon Academy. Founded in 2005, Beacon Academy believes in starting early. Each year, it funds a "jump year" for a small group of bright, motivated, Boston-area eighth graders from lower-resourced school districts. Jump Year enables these students to acquire the academic, social, and emotional tools they need to earn scholarships at competitive independent high schools around New England and achieve success in high school, college, and in their first careers.

There are many internships, university-based assistantships, and unpaid career development opportunities that will help with building your self-awareness during these starter career acts.

Formal education as starter career acts. While minimum wage jobs in tuxedo shops and computer resellers provide you with insight and experience, they are temporary and should not be your sole focus at this stage. Your formal education should take precedence, whatever that means to you. Your education should be paramount at this stage, whether an apprenticeship program, a certificate program, a training course, or a degree achieved at a university. Whatever you decide, education is needed at this initial stage. Low-wage unrelated experiences, while illuminating, are not enough to move you to the next phase. Even McDonald's offers business skills training at their Hamburger University, with campuses worldwide (no drive-through classrooms, though).

Let's consider these recognizable examples:

- Ben Cohen and Jerry Greenfield completed a correspondence course from Penn State University in the 1970s on how to make ice cream. Their ice cream company, Ben & Jerry's, creates frozen desserts that are still enjoyed around the world today.

- Singer and actress Stefani Joanne Angelina Germanotta attended New York University's Tisch School and became the superstar we now know as Lady Gaga.

- The famous award-winning chef and TV host Bobby Flay attended the French Culinary Institute in New York City (now the International Culinary Center). After he completed the program, he worked for an established chef for three years before starting his first restaurant.

As these examples illustrate, some form of formal education can be extremely helpful in this starter phase of your career. Attending an educational institution for training, a degree, or an advanced degree will always be the most direct path to a valuable starter career act. That said, we acknowledge that formal educational institutions are a costly investment (especially in the United States). Universities can often help their graduates gain employment opportunities that students could not possibly gain on their own. Universities can also create a professional network (through their career services and alumni) that would be out of reach without the institutional support.

In college, you will have the opportunity to gain knowledge, learn skills, hone abilities, and build the professional network to help in your first foundational career act in the next phase. Colleges and universities are rich in experiential and networking opportunities and unparalleled for accelerating professional growth and exploration. We are, as you might imagine, very supportive of formal educational programs at colleges and universities.

Even though we are big fans of formal education, we also recognize that even the best university cannot *create* your ideal career for you. Education is not a passive process. To illustrate, ask a college student (or ask yourself if you are a college student): "What are your tuition dollars buying?" The answer tends to fall into one of three categories.

The first category of answers will describe how the degree is a first step in a chosen career act. As educated consumers, they are especially savvy. They have likely researched placement rates (and can probably recite how their university stacks up to others). Universities with highly ranked degree programs in the student's chosen field are always the best bet for those in this group because they have the best relationships with prospective employers and top graduate schools or professional schools. Students can network with the best in their chosen field (alums and professors) from day one of their college experience. With tenacity and a willingness to work hard, the path to their foundational career act is paved.

Not every college student falls into this laser-focused group, however. Another group of college students (who do not yet know what their ideal career will be) are not bashful about using their college years to learn about and explore their options. As educated consumers, the savvy ones in this group are willing to attend every possible career night, network with faculty members, network with alumni, network with guest speakers, audit classes (just because they sound interesting), join clubs, intern, network with fellow classmates, and pursue just about everything to squeeze the most out of their college experience. They might change their major many times but, ultimately, they will get their money's worth and walk away from their college experience with insight into how they like to work, what comes naturally, and the ideal career they want to start pursuing.

We don't worry about the first (laser-focused) or the second (exploring) group of college students. We worry about the third group, who tend to stumble into a major, have little engagement with the university for career development, and graduate with a degree they can't quite figure out how to use in a field that does not excite them very much. They might enjoy the social aspect of their college experience, but don't use it to explore their career options. They know more about the football team's statistics than they know about what's on the next statistics test (unless they're taking Statistics for Football Fans, in which case they're on their way to an A). After graduation, they take a job out of necessity when student loans start to become due (or their parents want them to get into the "real world"). They tend to wonder whether their degree was worth it. The exploration opportunities available in their college years slipped away—unused.

College education has many financial and professional advantages. The Bureau of Labor Statistics found that people who held a bachelor's degree had a weekly income of $1,305, about 60 percent more than those with a high school diploma.[2] Keeping in mind that correlation is not causation, you'll still need to squeeze as much professional development as possible from your college experience to see the maximum returns. If you are in this starter career act phase, we encourage you to adopt the behaviors of the first or second group—or wait a few years to go to college and use those pre-college years to explore some options so you can return to school with greater certainty and motivation. You don't want to get to graduation week and realize you really wanted to take that course in How to Make Ice Cream.

SKILLS TO GAIN DURING THIS PHASE

The dominant skills we want you to gain at this phase are *objective self-awareness* and a *tolerance of ambiguity*.

Objective self-awareness. With objectivity, you can have a greater self-awareness of your talents and reactions to work situations without prejudging how you *should* feel. This is helpful as people with greater self-awareness are more likely to see their role in their success and have higher levels of self-esteem.[3] Being able to see (and take credit for) your role in your success will help you see how you can steer your career. To gain objective self-awareness during your starter career acts, try the following:

1. Ask managers, instructors, or colleagues who have served you in a variety of work situations whether they see a pattern in what you do well (and not so well).

2. Whenever your performance on a task is less than stellar, identify the skills you need to improve your success on this task.

3. Identify situations at work in which you have the strongest reactions, whether positive or negative—specifically around those situations in which you seem to succeed (and not).

Tolerance of ambiguity. The next skill we want you to build is a *tolerance of ambiguity*. We encourage you to push your limits in this phase to try many new work-related experiences and in doing so increase your tolerance of ambiguity. Uncertainty is appropriate in this phase, if you use the time to learn about your work preferences—and having a higher level of tolerance of ambiguity enables you to embrace this phase.

Your tolerance of ambiguity will keep you from being swayed by those around you who are pushing you to certainty before you are ready. With a greater ability to handle uncertainty you will make a greater number of exploration-based choices, even when those choices might seem to "lack focus" to parents, friends, and advisors. For example, if you accept a low-level or low-paid position to learn about an industry, network, gain some exposure for an occupation, or develop the knowledge, skills, and abilities needed for the future, then these are exactly the starter career acts you will need. These starter career acts will eventually lead to your foundational career act (up next) but, to others, might seem random in their diversity. This is OK, provided the diverse experiences are moving you closer to clarity on your career journey. When well-meaning Aunt Gladys rolls her eyes at your choice, take a deep breath, and talk about the weather.

YOUR MINDSET DURING THIS PHASE

This is the phase in which many people establish their relationships with their careers. We want your mindset to be one of *career control*. Please do not let anyone tell you to think of this phase as "doing your time" or "paying your dues." While, admittedly, starter career acts might not be the most stimulating, comments like these can be detrimental because they socialize people into career passivity. You have more power than you realize to determine your next steps—especially as you advance your skills.

Phase 2: Foundational career acts

At this stage, you have likely identified what you think will be an ideal career. You have likely completed career acts such as a degree, apprenticeship, certificate, or training program. You may have a few lines of experience on your resume from internships and part-time jobs. Congratulations! You are now ready to start your foundational career acts.

For many, foundational career acts begin with their first full-time professional job, the first intentional step toward their ideal career, often just after graduation from a degree or certificate program. Whether you are a new graduate, a career changer, or a late entrant to a professional career, your primary goal at this phase is to maximize your energy and enthusiasm to gather high-quality professional experiences quickly. You are like the plane taxiing down a runway, gaining speed for take-off.

At this stage you should experiment with unconventional opportunities that will accelerate your professional development toward a specific career goal. This could mean working in a start-up, accepting a role in a different part of the country (or world), or engaging in a job where you can learn a specific skill needed for your ideal career. We encourage you to accept the positions that will give you the best opportunity to grow your skill base and further clarify an ideal career with the best and most diverse experiences.

In this phase (and every phase), you may reframe, refine, or even change your ideal career by exercising your self-curiosity and testing your interests—even with things that may seem outlandish. Changing your path is not a problem, provided you are doing it with intention and control.

SELECTING FOUNDATIONAL CAREER ACTS

While tempting, do not select your first job based solely on salary and/or a marquee company name. Paula followed her gut after finishing her PhD. Her top two academic job offers were from very different universities; one was a public state university offering a lower salary and the other was a Top 10 business school in a prestigious private university offering a higher salary. *Which one did she select?* The public university. While not as well-paid, the public university offered amazing colleagues who would support and mentor, opportunities to work abroad (which was key for her international area), and teaching experiences that would offer a stretch challenge from day one. (For the first few years her masters' students were, on average, older than she was.) She flourished in that environment and her career accelerated in ways she could not have replicated at the more "logical" choice.

Andy took a bit of a winding path in this phase. After graduating from college, his primary passion was playing rugby, and he worked as a computer programmer to support his rugby-playing habit. After being injured, he took on leadership roles in rugby as the President of the Boston Rugby Football Club. His mentor in work, Jim McHugh, inspired him to pursue his interests, seeing him (and helping him see himself) as a "tech-savvy businessperson." Mind and heart now set on a career in technology, Andy went to business school for an MBA. His essay for the business school application was about how difficult it was managing the various personalities of the rugby players on the Boston Rugby Club. A great lesson in how one career act can enable and inform the next!

At that time, Andy was newly married with a young daughter, and with the inspiration of his mentor and business school professor Phil Anderson he resisted the typical path for MBA graduates, which would be a high-paying job at a consulting firm or Wall Street investment firm (which he viewed as potentially soulless work). Instead, Andy and his young family picked up and moved to Austin, Texas, where he accepted a salesperson/jack-of-all-trades job for an AI software start-up called Trilogy. He was inspired largely by conversations with the founders and start-up team that suggested he'd have an opportunity to carve his own path and resurrect his interest in artificial intelligence. (And he did.) When the company spun off a piece of its business, Andy went with the start-up to get hands-on experience in founding a start-up; in this case, meeting ambitious revenue goals. (Which he achieved.) He later went on to help found a new start-up back in New England. It was becoming clear to Andy (and everyone who knew him) that during every new act, he sought more and more risk in all his projects and lifestyle. This set the tone for the rest of his career: he was effective at starting new companies from scratch, often from an academic project or idea.

Both of us took unexpected paths in this foundational phase relying on objective self-awareness and tolerance of ambiguity we formed in our starter phase. Unfortunately, too many people languish in their careers at this foundational phase. The reason is often because they settle too quickly, based on income or prestige associated with their company or job title. Income and prestige are seductive. They lure you into relinquishing control over your career. Before you know it, they are in charge and taking you places you don't want to go. Talking about your impressive-sounding job may impress everybody at your class reunion, but deep down you know there's somewhere else you want to be. Let's talk about why this happens.

A high salary is not a bad thing, but it could place you on a hedonic treadmill too soon which is problematic.[4] It usually happens like this: You start to make money. You buy nice cars, clothes, furniture, etc. They make you happy for a short period of time until you grow accustomed to them. You look to acquire even nicer things and the treadmill continues; your stale, higher-paying job feeds the insatiable beast that eats through your money, taking control over your career.

Please don't misinterpret this. We too like nice things. They are, well, nicer than cheap material things. But, in this phase, we encourage you to reframe the assessment of your professional success in terms of great developmental experiences, *not material things*. If you live below your means in this phase, you will have more degrees of freedom to make better career choices later in your career. Off-the-rack today, custom-fit tomorrow.

Like a high salary, working for a popular, highly desirable, and well-respected company is not a bad thing, per se. Large, mature, and well-known organizations can place their best and brightest employees, otherwise known as their stars and high potentials (HiPo), into robust career paths. Being identified in this group is a good thing. After all, it is nice to be called a "star." More than a label, being a part of this group showers you with accelerated career advancement, better exposure to executive mentors, more rewarding stretch assignments, high-profile projects, and increased visibility.[5] Nice. But, like all golden handcuffs, all this love comes at a cost. Being in this elite group of talent feels prestigious, but in doing so, you just relinquished your career decisions to the organization that needs to primarily leverage your skills for wealth creation.

Being a part of a high-potential career path has lulled many into believing they have embarked on the right career journey. In many cases, unless they have a very clear line from entry-level to their ideal career, the opposite has just occurred. They gave up control of their career journey. It is not as though they have stopped thinking about career moves. Rather, their options are hyper-focused on only the roles in which the company needs their skills—and not where they need to build for their future ideal career. It works when the path the company offers and the path the "star" wants are the same. For everyone else, the results are not as fulfilling. It's like asking your mom to pick a tattoo design: even if she has great taste in tats, it's not yours.

You don't even need to be labeled a "star" or "high potential" for this to occur. As we noted earlier in the book, too many people join companies believing that they have landed on the first rung of a long-term career ladder. They erroneously believe that the company will steady that ladder, so to speak, so they can easily climb, promotion after promotion, to achieve their ideal career. They buy into the myth that the first job will give them an opportunity for long-term employment. Long-term, steady, and satisfying employment with a single company is, for most, an artifact of the past. At this phase of your career, you should take risks, build your network, and gain experiences that will build your knowledge, skills, and abilities.

Let's dig into this myth of the career ladder a bit more, using a concrete example. For high-performing business school graduates at top colleges and universities, a popular professional path has been to go to work at McKinsey, Bain, or another prestigious consulting firm upon graduation. Consulting firms offer the promise of working with lots of companies and projects while learning from senior partners and other mentors—a good thing, right? Unfortunately, once you've been proven particularly good at something, you'll often be pigeonholed to stay in that lane. As a consultant, you are gaining experience but not necessarily developing your ability to execute tangible results. Many consultants we've known look back on their careers and feel like they have spent decades generating meaningless slide decks that never result in tangible results from their work—and feel rather empty in their contributions to society.

Regardless of the company you join, whether in consulting or any other field, remember that career progression is optimized for the company's bottom line, not your personal development. If those career paths align with your ideal career, then there is a win-win. Go for it! For most people, however, this is not the case, and they relinquish their control too quickly at this stage.

Make this foundational phase—finances permitting—the time to take some risks and learn what is most fulfilling. Consider these when selecting foundational career acts:

1. Don't over-optimize salary and prestigious company name. Try not to be swayed by those who are pushing you in a career direction solely for financial reasons. This is your career to manage.

2. Use your judgment, ask questions diplomatically about developmental opportunities available.

3. Seek out and use your personal mentors to see what they would recommend you select based on your ideal career goals.

4. Don't be afraid to change to a new job once the one you are in is clearly not helping you move forward in your career journey. There is always a balance between staying in a role long enough to not appear like a flaky employee to a reasonable person and making a strategic career move.

5. Whatever job you pursue, be intentional, commit to being excellent in the role, and *learn* while you are in the position.

6. Don't fear failure. It's always easier to start back on the ladder when you've only slipped off the bottom rung.

Let's give you the example of Kelsey Cole, one of Andy's mentees. When Kelsey was a newly minted liberal arts grad with a passion for rugby and an interest in technology, he took a sales job with an industry research firm. While he learned a lot quickly about his industry of interest and how to sell, the job wasn't stimulating enough for him. He mined his professional network, Andy included, a fellow rugby enthusiast, to create an apprenticeship opportunity: running operations for Koa Labs, Andy's (at that time, new) investment portfolio. Today, Kelsey is a leader in the Customer Success team for Tamr, Inc., a critical front-line position that uses his prodigious energy, brains, and take-charge personality to make customers successful in using the company's products.

Like Kelsey, you might need to ask for—and even create—your opportunities at this phase. You are still an unknown so you will need to perfect your pitch, your clear articulation of what you would like to do, what you can offer the organization, and what developmental opportunities you hope to receive in return. You are selling yourself to obtain the role you most want. If that sounds icky and self-promoting, focus on the fact that the company will also benefit from your motivation, commitment, and skills. Focus on the "win-win."

SKILLS TO GAIN DURING THIS PHASE

Gaining technical or tangible skills (i.e., knowledge, skills, and abilities) which will be needed for your ideal career is the overarching goal in this phase. You might have raw talent or natural ability, but your skills, in this phase, will need to be honed with practical experience. In addition to the technical or tangible skills you are gaining, there are two more valuable skills we would like you to acquire during this stage: *self-advocacy* and *how to make graceful exits*.

Self-advocacy. The foundational phase is about building and honing skills through rich learning experiences. To do this you will need to learn *self-advocacy*. If you are a strong self-advocate, you can have open and assertive (but not aggressive) conversations with your manager about the skills you hope to gain while in the role and future opportunities you want to experience. Here are some ways to build this skill of self-advocacy for your career.

- **Communicate your goals openly, clearly, and effectively.** When asking for new opportunities, do not do this with a sense of entitlement, rather, from the perspective of self-development. You could try: "I am interested in doing more of [new opportunity]. Would you have any suggestions for what I should start doing today to make me eligible for [new opportunity] in the future?"

- **Take initiative and ask for opportunities.** Don't wait for opportunities to come to you—seek them out. If you see an opening for a new project or job opportunity, express your interest and qualifications. This might seem a bit awkward if you are someone who would rather quietly do your job and wait to be recognized. In fairness to your organization, however, how would any manager know that you want more if you don't express that desire? Even if you are not granted the request, you are still practicing the important skill of advocating for yourself. Research found that employees who take more initiative build better relationships with their supervisors and enjoy better career success.[6]

- **Be realistic about your skills.** Before advocating for yourself, it is important to have some self-awareness around your strengths and weaknesses—and be able to communicate them both comfortably. Conveying the skills you would like to develop will show your manager that you aren't making the request casually. You know your weaknesses and are making the request with those in mind. Also, don't be shy about conveying your skills in which you excel, especially those your manager might not see but are needed for the role you are requesting.

- **Be persistent and ask again.** Advocating for yourself can sometimes be a long and challenging process. It's important to be proactive and persistent, even if your requests are not immediately granted.

Continue to demonstrate that you are ready for the next challenge by proactively working on your skills. Your persistence is often rewarded. Research has found that having a proactive personality is related to greater salary, more promotions, and higher overall career satisfaction.[7] Most people see greater salary, more promotions, and higher overall career satisfaction as good things (not sure we need research to confirm that).

Graceful exits. During this foundational phase, it is a good time to practice and hone your skill of *graceful exits*. When you have this skill, you can transition from one project to another, one employer to another, one manager to another with everyone feeling good about the move and even happy for you. You are charming in your exit, respectful, and grateful to those who gave you an opportunity to grow and develop. These graceful transitions are not easy: the ability to make them effectively is like building a muscle. The more graceful transitions you make, the more muscle you'll build.

One of Andy's favorite examples of a graceful exit was when a young, up-and-coming superstar, Eliot Knudsen, came to him and said, "I'm going to leave for another job at a different company. You tell me, Andy, when would be the best time to make the move. You've invested in me and my development and I want to make sure that the impact of my departure on the company is minimized in the process." Eliot made a graceful exit and this approach aligned Andy to Eliot's side. Andy remains one of Eliot's biggest fans.

Here are some ways to build the skill of making graceful transitions:

- **Appreciate that your transition will be disruptive.** A key principle when making these changes is to give your existing manager and company the time required to adjust when you leave. We've always found that the more time and advance notice given to the people for whom we have worked, the better the transition for us and for our previous company, boss, and mentors. This is antithetical to the principle of "at will" employment in the US but is one of the practices that the most successful people do—no matter what the "legal requirement" might be. For most situations, "submitting your two weeks" notice is *not* considered a graceful exit. Neither is breaking the news by email, text, or a Tik Tok happy dance.

- **Show gratitude for what you have learned.** Every career act can be a situation to learn and grow. Especially when someone helped you develop, be generous with your words of appreciation when you announce your departure. If you have a hard time saying it, write it. For example, this is the note Paula sent to her colleagues when she made the decision to change universities:

Dear Colleagues,

As most of you know, this will be my last semester at [UNIVERSITY], a decision that was extremely difficult for me to make. For almost two decades I have been comfortably ensconced in the support of colleagues I admire, in the reflected glory of the world's best HRM department, and in the love of some I count among my closest friends.

My gratitude is limitless for my past and present colleagues who trusted me with stretch challenges, guided me with their counsel, and collaborated with me on programs and projects. I grew up at [UNIVERSITY].

As difficult as the decision was, I am excited to be joining [DIFFERENT UNIVERSITY] as the [NEW JOB TITLE] where I will be starting [NEW OPPORTUNITY]. I am thrilled to have the opportunity once more to roll up my sleeves, build, and lead.

Please wish me luck in this next chapter of my career.

With deep appreciation,
Paula

YOUR MINDSET DURING THIS PHASE

In this foundational phase, your mindset needs to be one of *self-focus*, hyper-attentive to your development and professional growth. We are not suggesting you become self-centered or self-absorbed. In fact, just the opposite. In this phase you should be a grateful professional sponge, so to speak, absorbing every professional experience with commitment to excellence. Through your dedication, your organization's leaders will see you as receptive to feedback and appreciative for opportunities. Based on your commitment to excellence, they will listen to you when you advocate for more.

There is a nuance here. While we want you to commit to excellence in every role you are given, we don't want you to feel overly obligated to stay in your role or remain with the organization out of misplaced loyalty. For most people, a job during this phase is *part* of the journey, not the end goal. At the start of a new job, try to determine the developmental goal and, after achieving it (and staying long enough to demonstrate excellence in your technical skills), plan for the exit. The exit might be to a different company or to a different role within the company.

This self-focus mindset is not the most natural. Many people work hard through starter career acts to land their first job but, once in it, allow corporate "powers" to take over, relinquishing control to the organization that gave them a chance. Ouch. Bad strategy. Remember the major theme of this book: You are in control of your career *throughout* the journey, not just the first phase. You will need to chart your course into—and out of—career acts to get closer to having more of what you really want from your life and your career.

To build self-focus on your professional development during this phase, try the following:

1. Ask for additional roles. Engage in those opportunities that will give you greater knowledge or help build the skills and abilities needed for the future. If you are very new in your career, additional tasks might help you gain a better sense for the way you like to work.

2. Volunteer for tasks that will give you exposure and help you build the knowledge, skills, and abilities you need.

3. Seek a mentor who has already "made it" in your ideal career act. Ideally, find a mentor who is open to giving critical advice and feedback.

4. Demonstrate your commitment to the industry, field, company, and role to learn and earn the respect of others in your network.

5. Be attentive, excellent, and engaged to gain the most from the experiences you are offered.

Another key feature of your mindset during this phase is to have a *growth mindset*. Carol Dweck[8] coined the phrase to describe how people best develop by having a commitment to learning and a willingness to risk failing when trying a stretch challenge. Through trial they learn and through resilience they grow. The growth mindset is far more desirable than the fixed mindset, which fosters the need to look smart and correct, diminishing the number of risks one takes in a hope to appear perfect. The fixed mindset stalls people in their career because they can remain doing what they have always done well without risks of making mistakes.

With your growth mindset, you should get out of your comfort zone and engage in stretch assignments to test and develop your skills. Keep checking in with yourself on whether you have inadvertently slipped into a fixed mindset. For some, as they become more accomplished, their confidence allows career inertia to set in, less willing to take a chance at bruising an ego. Research has found that when you have a growth mindset, you are more likely to enjoy higher engagement at work, have better performance, and have greater satisfaction.[9]

These foundational career acts should be full of opportunities to learn, gain skills, and hone (or change) opportunities to move closer to your ideal career. At this phase, we want you to explore, grow, and learn everything you can possibly learn. In this spirit, you are (as always) staying in control of your professional development and not letting go of the reins.

Phase 5: High-growth career acts

High-growth career acts are the roles you select to reflect both your professional identity and reputation (i.e., how others see you within your profession, industry, or field). You'll know you have moved to the high-growth career phase when you start receiving inquiries for employment from headhunters and colleagues from different organizations. People are interested in hiring you for your marketable skills and abilities. You have a budding professional network and the foundation of your professional reputation. During this phase, you might even have the skills and resources to start an entrepreneurial venture or to add an additional income-generating career act.

Put your seatbelt on. In this phase, your career and your life are about to pick up speed and the road might have a few hairpin turns. For many people, their personal lives have become richer, fuller, and often more complicated during this phase. For example, you might start a family, drop roots into a community, and buy a home. If these happen, your career journey shares time with making sure your children finish their homework, your lawn is mowed, and you don't forget your anniversary.

Recalling this high-growth phase of his career, a successful friend of ours once quipped, "When I started my career, I had lots of time and no money. Now I have lots of money and no time. I think there was a day in between." We agree. We can't remember that day either. Whatever your path and life responsibilities are, in this high-growth phase of your career, **your time is your most precious resource**.

SELECTING HIGH-GROWTH CAREER ACTS

In this phase, we want you to use your accumulated experiences to find *great* high-growth career opportunities. You will select career acts that have the greatest positive impact on your professional identity. It is critical to become selective about which opportunities you pursue because more will start to open, and it is easy to get pulled in the wrong direction. Many people in this phase find themselves on an incremental promotional career ladder within an organization, even though the most impactful next step might be to take a role with a different organization.

We just need a reality check reminder on promotions. Promotions are wonderful, a reason to open that bottle of champagne stored in your refrigerator. *Everyone likes the dopamine hit from being recognized for a job well-done.* Please remember, however, that you are being recognized for *what you can offer the organization* and not necessarily *what is ideal for you.* If those two are in alignment, as before, this is great news—and we are happy for you. Just be certain that your decision to accept any promotion is *intentional* and not by default. As the flight attendants say: "Look around. The nearest exit might be behind you." Look around. The next step might be at another organization. Yes, the promotion offer may be the proverbial bird in the hand, but if you look around just a little you may find that there are bushels of better birds waiting for you.

In this phase, leadership opportunities will also start to present themselves. These too can be enticing but might not be right for you just yet. If you have mastered all the technical and tangible skills you need for your ideal career, leadership skills are important to acquire. Many people move into leadership before they are ready—before they have reached the level of excellence in their critical and unique tangible skills. Sometimes it is better to acquire leadership skills through a community or volunteer organization while using your employment experience to further develop the technical skills you could not acquire elsewhere.

In this phase, it is important not to undershoot. Decisions made in this phase can change your life because they affect your professional identity. Resist the need to please your boss or impress your family and friends. If they look at you strangely and ask, "Why would you ever want to do the thing that will be fulfilling and help you reach your long-term goals when you can have a corner office now?" just smile and talk about the weather. Make the decisions that will best position you to take the next and most direct steps on your career journey. For example, Andy moved off the technology executive leadership path to go into a hands-on IT job at a biopharmaceutical company. He did this to learn the industry. Similarly, Andy's friend Francis deSouza went from a technology start-up founder to a position at a multi-billion-dollar software company. This unexpected move prepared him to next run a billion-dollar biomedical company. Both Francis and Andy made what seemed to be counter-intuitive decisions on the surface. In both cases though, they were the critical decisions to acquire their skills that would move them each to their ideal careers respectively.

SKILLS TO GAIN DURING THIS PHASE

In this high-growth phase, we want you to build your *intentionality* muscle. To do this you need to commit to your career decisions as deliberate moves on a path toward an ideal career. While every change was intentional up to this point, we want you to be an order-of-magnitude more intentional about your career choices in this phase. This isn't a dry run. Your professional reputation is forming. Eyes are on you.

In this phase, we hope you feel a sense of agency over your career options and choices. If you are on the career journey you most want, you will feel empowered by a job change. If you still haven't locked in on your career destination, you might feel anxious to leave something secure. It is a good test.

Let's consider Krishna Yeshwant's career journey in this phase. With a BS in computer science from a prestigious university, Krishna became a programmer and helped start two technology companies that were later acquired by larger companies. Krishna went on to join a new Silicon Valley venture capital firm, helping identify new companies for investments. To increase his skills, he earned an MBA in the process. In his late thirties, still not locked in on the ideal career, he followed his growing interest in medicine and started a new career act: he became a doctor.

Does Krishna's journey sound a bit crazy? We wouldn't call it crazy—more like radical intentionality, especially given the commitment involved in getting a medical degree. He practiced medicine at a leading teaching hospital for several years—before turning his focus on running the firm's investments in the burgeoning area of biopharmaceuticals. Krishna got there. He achieved his ideal career. Like Krishna, we want you to get there too, maybe with radical intentionality to make nontraditional moves—or maybe with the courage to make the choices needed.

To build your intentionality for high-growth career acts, try these:

1. When you are ready to take on a new role, network into as many possible opportunities as you can—being certain to learn what each opportunity can offer you. You might be surprised to learn your value when you learn of your possible opportunities.

2. Be certain you understand what the new opportunities will offer with respect to enhancing your professional skills, reputation, and network.

3. Identify all the personal and professional priorities you have and seek to maximize all aspects of your life. Remember that time is your most precious resource at this stage.

4. Communicate your expectations and needs before you accept a new role. If you have multiple career acts or nonwork priorities, you need to be certain the new potential role works with the other aspects of your life.

5. Ignore those in your life space who are heightening your anxiety without knowledge (e.g., those who say, "why would you ever leave ABC company?"). Listen only to the advice of those who know the steps you will need to move closer to your ideal career in the role you are in.

YOUR MINDSET DURING THIS PHASE

In this phase your dominant mindset is *a commitment to your purpose*—your time, money, and energy need to be purposefully leveraged to advance your life in the direction you most desire. To foster this mindset, you will need to lock in on the ideals you most want in your personal and professional life. Every decision, whenever possible, needs to facilitate—or at least not deter—your path toward that goal.

There are five ways to foster a commitment to your purpose mindset:

1. Focus on the high-impact activities and begin to shed other things. To learn more about how to adhere to this mindset, we recommend the book *The ONE Thing: The Surprisingly Simple Truth About Extraordinary Results* by Gary Keller and Jay Papasan.[10] In this book, they encourage all of us to start each day with the question "What's the One Thing I can do, such that by doing it everything else will be easier or unnecessary?" Make this question a habit.

2. Say "no" to everything that is not essential. We want you to become comfortable saying "no" to every ego-stroking and guilt-forming new opportunity offered to you. It doesn't come naturally to most of us, so you may want to practice in front of a mirror or with your dog or cat. We want you to get so comfortable at saying "no" that your knee-jerk default is "no." This mindset will provide the time most of us need to pause to think through how the opportunity fits into your broader plan for your career, family, resources, etc. To motivate this mindset, we recommend the book *Essentialism: The Disciplined Pursuit of Less*.[11] In it, Greg McKeown challenges us to examine every decision with the question: "Is this essential?" If the answer is "no," do not engage.

3. Say "yes" to quality time with loved ones. We want you to preserve your limited time to be fully present in the relationships with your family and close friends. Without sounding harsh, everyone in your life does not deserve the same level of attention your loved ones deserve. If you are a people pleaser, you might experience a swirl of guilt-based emotions such as: *Am I letting my team down by not planning the holiday party again this year?* Or: *Will my friend be upset*

that I am not attending his kid's eighth birthday party? Chances are the answer is "no" provided you are open about your availability. Our advice: Send a gift to the eight-year-old and have coffee with your friend.

4. Say "yes" to expanding your network. We encourage you to say "yes" to opportunities to meet people and foster relationships through mentorship and networking. Your positive reputation is transmitted through others, and you learn about opportunities and gain insights about your field by cultivating these important relationships.

5. Recognize your ideal future and then think of every decision as an incremental step toward your ideal future state. This means that in every decision, both large and small, ask yourself: *Will the choice I am making now help me thrive in the future?* In addition to this helping your career, it will also help your well-being. *Will this donut for breakfast help me thrive in the future?* No. *Will making time for the gym help me thrive in the future?* Yes. Commit to trying this for even one week and see how your behavior changes.

Phase 4: High-focus career acts

Congratulations! You have made it to the high-focus career act phase. At this phase, you are as close as most will come to achieving an ideal career. In this phase, you might even have multiple career acts comprising your career portfolio. You know you are in this phase because you are in-demand and have earned the confidence associated with that distinction. You have cultivated a valuable professional niche, a positive reputation, and a unique set of skills that are difficult to replicate.

If you have an entrepreneurial energy, at this phase you have likely leveraged your skills to start some type of business that has started to grow such that others might be working for you. As an entrepreneur, in this phase you are growing your business, organizational culture, and employees such that your values, methods, and skills are reflected in them. You see yourself in your business, so to speak.

SELECTING HIGH-FOCUS CAREER ACTS

In this high-focus stage, the professional world has figured out your value and, hopefully, you also know your worth. You're the whole package, and you're crushing it in your field because you have the skills most never took the time to cultivate. You can enjoy a bit of a swagger during this phase. You earned it.

Since you possess critical and unique skills, you can likely identify the situations in which they are most valuable. This might mean taking a high-focus role in an organization where you can have the greatest level of desired influence, or it might mean growing your entrepreneurial venture. It might mean both. The bottom line in selecting career acts in this high-focus phase is to, possibly, rethink of your ideal career as an *ideal career portfolio*, where you invest your time and money in the career acts that will provide you with the greatest overall return in personal and professional fulfillment.

Wait a minute. Did we just change the goal from an ideal career to a career portfolio? Sort of, yes. We have found that many people get to this stage of their careers and realize that they have skills and capacity to apply their talents across multiple career acts. Each career act within an ideal career portfolio provides a different fulfilling piece of that overall ideal career. For others though, one great career act is all they need. In their career portfolio, they have the metaphorical purchase of Apple stock in 1980.

SKILLS TO GAIN DURING THIS PHASE

In this phase, you should work on mastering your *leadership skills*. In addition to enjoying the pinnacle of success, honor the fact that you are likely in a leadership role, whether tangibly with direct reports or as a professional whom others wish to emulate. You are now a role model, a mentor, and a motivational exemplar who can have a strong influence on the organizations you grow and the teams you lead. Go ahead and call yourself an "influencer" (just don't call your employees "followers").

Providing advice on how to improve your leadership skills would fill volumes. There are entire academic journals dedicated to the topic and countless books filled with sage advice from those who have led through extraordinary circumstances, from ancient to modern. Without any attempt to be comprehensive, our top seven pieces of leadership advice are:

1. **Act exactly as you want everyone in your organization to act.** If you act like a jerk, this will be socialized into others as an acceptable way to behave. As a leader, you are a socializing agent for others within your organization because their eyes are on you. Don't be a jerk.

2. **Balance your strategic vision with humility for the unknown.** People will gravitate to you for your confidence and vision. However, in today's highly complex, uncertain, and competitive world, you cannot possibly have all the answers. Create an environment where people can speak truth to power and offer other possible solutions, approaches, etc. without fear of retribution.

3. **Hold others accountable but don't be a control freak.** Everyone appreciates freedom to choose their course of action. We all value autonomy. As numerous research studies have found, it is motivating.[12] That said, make sure everyone who works for you has the resources, tools, training, and instructions they need to be successful. Make sure you give clear guidance for what success and high performance would entail—and hold people to those standards.

4. **Create a sense of belonging.** Everyone likes to feel like they are part of the team, the tribe—as interconnected as they want to be to others

within the organization. Research has found that, across many studies, a sense of belonging will increase employees' motivation.[13] This does not mean that you require your team members to attend happy hours or bowling nights. It just means that you create a connection, a spirit of "us" in which employees want to affiliate. We recommend that you encourage helpfulness among your team members so they garner a sense that others on the team have their back and will help if needed—and they have theirs. Everyone knows there's no "I" in "team," but there are quite a few in "maximizing facilitation."

5. **Create a sense of purpose.** Regardless of level, provide every member on your team with a sense of the bigger picture—a connection to the clients served, the ways the product is used, greater purpose and the like. Take the time to do this well and create meaning. In meta-analyses, having the sense of meaningful work is related to your employees' engagement, commitment, job satisfaction, and willingness to remain with your organization.[14] Having a sense of purpose and meaning is especially true now that some from your team might be working from home. While working from home is desirable for many, be certain you are not asking your employees to do a job in isolation (no sense of belonging) without any connection to a greater purpose.

6. **Mentor.** Mentoring really means getting to know what makes a person tick and helping them sort out a path to leverage their own talents and motivations. This doesn't mean creating someone in your own image, encouraging them to do what you have done in your career. Help them find their unique path. Research has found that your mentorship will help your mentees feel more confident in their career decisions and enhance their confidence in their career moves.[15]

7. **Create your professional legacy.** Now is the time to create the impact for which you will be remembered, your professional legacy.

This legacy might be related to a tangible accomplishment. It could also be related to how you conducted yourself as a leader or a role model. We can all remember a former manager whom we remember fondly for their character, values, vision, and leadership. Your legacy is forming at this stage because you are directly and indirectly affecting the lives of many. Work in a way that is both consistent with your values and how you would like to be remembered in the future.

YOUR MINDSET AT THIS PHASE

In this phase, *knowing your professional worth and power* are paramount. When you know your professional worth, you have a deep understanding of the situations in which your skills are unique and when your talents are critical for achieving wealth for yourself and the organizations you join or build as an entrepreneur. If you become over-confident at this phase, you will likely be surprised that the world does not value you as highly as you value yourself. We have observed that more people are *under*-confident at this phase, underselling their uniqueness and the value they bring. For them, this phase is the time to stop hiding their light under a bushel before it catches fire and burns the whole barn down.

In this phase, you will need to accept the power you now have. Your power might be ascribed to your position if you are a founder, owner, or senior leader. Then again, your power might not be reflected in your level on the company's org chart. Your power might be soft, based on your technical expertise, your role as an influencer, or your stellar reputation within your industry. With soft power, people go to you because they know you know things others don't. They go to you because they know you know people and are well respected.

Whether in a position power or soft power, we want you to have a mindset of knowing your power and, of course, using it well. You can accomplish this by being a source of great advice and being generous with your knowledge. You'll create positive ripples in any situation in which you can provide your professional influence. Being a good citizen in the organization and a good leader for your team will continue to add to your credibility, engagement, and reach. In addition to the professional benefits, it feels good to enhance the work life of others, adding to your overall work fulfillment.

Phase 5: Giving-back career acts

In this phase, you use your accumulated experiences, skills, and abilities to give back to others. If you are in this phase, **you have made it**, and will likely feel fulfilled in your career. If you are already at this phase, you are probably giving career advice to others and not likely reading this book (but, we hope, recommending it). Even if you are far from this phase of your career, it is still worth discussing for a preview of the wonderful last leg that your well-directed career journey can have.

When you think about people at this stage, you might be thinking there isn't more to do in their career. It is time to retire. Buy a tracksuit and take up whittling. If this is your conception of the final phase of your career, then think again. There is one more phase of your career journey—and this one will likely be your best and most fulfilling.

When you are at the top with an ideal career, you aren't really striving to move up anymore as you were in the high-focus phase. In this phase, you are no longer leveraging your skills to advance yourself or your organizations. Rather, you are sharing your skills with others to help them build *their* careers. You are actively involved in mentoring, teaching, and coaching for others to achieve. With greater financial success, you can share your wealth by becoming an angel investor or a philanthropist to accelerate others through their own career journeys.

People who have achieved this level of their career journey are now happily looking outward, identifying ways to use their talents to be a good citizen in the organization, community, industry, and the like.

At this stage, you might begin to invest in others with time or money and expand your reach. For example, in this phase, Andy established Koa Labs, "paying it forward" to make seed investments in promising technology and biotech companies. With several more start-ups under his personal belt and Koa invested in about one hundred companies, Andy channels seed investments to founders with technical backgrounds from traditionally under-capitalized communities, such as female founders, founders of color, and immigrant founders. Being able to use his skills and resources to see so many founders realize their own dreams has helped Andy achieve the pinnacle of his ideal career's journey.

In Paula's role as a university professor, there are ready-made opportunities to mentor junior colleagues, graduate students returning to school to advance their professional goals, and undergraduate students launching their careers. Every opportunity to mentor, even the brief "mentoring moments" at professional conferences, has provided her a way to codify her own skills while enjoying a helper's high along the way.

We are not alone in our ability to enjoy this state of our careers. Among our circle of friends, we have other diverse examples of those who are now "giving back":

- Don Bulens is a fixer-CEO who goes from company to company improving the companies, their leadership teams, and their organizational cultures along the way. He loves it and is successful, the hallmark of this high-focus phase.

- Deborah Daccord is one of Boston's leading attorneys, a partner in a prestigious law firm. Using her skills as a business professional and legal expert (and a serious foodie), she has invested in multiple female-chefs' restaurants. She has also served on the Board of Big Sisters of Boston and invests in women-owned businesses through Golden Seeds. Her skills at this stage have enabled others to succeed.

- Dana Born is a retired Brigadier General from the Air Force who has been able to use her stellar leadership acumen, honed after many years of being the Dean of the Air Force Academy, toward leadership development at the Harvard Kennedy School. She is also a Distinguished Fellow with the HOW Institute for Society to contribute to advancing moral leadership through various contributions, including serving on boards in this generative next chapter of her life and leadership.

- Rich Miner is a visionary technologist who co-invented a ubiquitously used piece of technology: Android, the mobile operating system later acquired by Google. Now, in the latter phases of his career, he has a few companies in motion and uses his resources to invest in and advise other inventors.

- John Lilly is a computer scientist who has balanced his technical positions with high-profile companies with his work in venture capital, along with a career-long act as a board advisor to start-ups and nonprofits. He's also a consulting assistant professor and lecturer at a prestigious university. (And an expert juggler of career acts, obviously.)

- With a career spanning three decades, choreographer/actor/director/producer Debbie Allen is still on her toes (metaphorically speaking). She's had great success and acclaim across all categories, receiving numerous awards for her work as well as four honorary doctorates. A former member of the President's Committee on the Arts and Humanities, Debbie was appointed by President George W. Bush to represent the United States as a Cultural Ambassador of Dance. In 2001, she opened the nonprofit Debbie Allen Dance Company in Los Angeles. With a focus on disenfranchised Black and Latino communities, DADA's faculty and staff use dance, theater, and performance to enrich, inspire, and transform the lives of students. Over her long career, Debbie has also served as a mentor to many young performers and a self-esteem champion to women and girls.

These diverse individuals remain highly engaged in their careers even as some approach what you might think of as their "retirement years." They are happily leveraging their skills to accelerate the careers and businesses of others—and feeling a great sense of fulfillment in the process. Each person we named has embraced mentorship as a central part of their careers. They've intentionally made mentorship, advising, and angel investing one or more of their career acts, providing a fulfilling apex to their career journeys.

Many (but not all) who reach this phase of their career are in their 60s, 70s, 80s, and beyond. The insight of those who are happily giving back is profound: don't stop engaging in your career when you reach the phase that most people think of as retirement. While much of the world believes that happiness in retirement means less professional engagement, it is not the case for many who have had fulfilling careers, provided they can engage with and mentor others in this phase. For them, riding off into the sunset means helping others find a new dawn.

Giving back accumulated experience in the form of shared wisdom is the greatest source of career fulfillment most have experienced. Engagement with others through give-back career acts will keep you socially connected, a feature of retirement that has been found to contribute to the retirement adjustment (an important feature of retirement, up there with features like physical health for the positive transition to retirement).[16]

SELECTING CAREER ACTS AT THIS PHASE

In this phase, we hope you will be in demand as a mentor, investor, or an advisor. Your opportunities at this phase need to be assessed just as they are at every other phase of your career—what will provide you with the greatest sense of fulfillment based on your unique desires, skills, goals, and talents. For example, some people like to teach once they reach retirement while others choose to mentor budding entrepreneurs. This act in your career is the most selfless, but in many ways the most rewarding when you select your opportunities with your own preferences in mind.

As you think about career acts at this phase, you can also think about what you want your legacy to be. For many people, they see their legacy in the eyes of their children and grandchildren. Others see their legacy as the companies they have created or the products they have invented. We want you to think about legacy in one other way—the positive influence you have had in helping shape the lives of others, who could not be where they are without you.

This all might be sounding like the closing scene of "It's a Wonderful Life," but it is true. As you ascend to this final phase of your career, select the career acts that will maximize what you like to do with who you most want to help. Once there, give yourself the time to take stock of the positive ripples you have set in motion in other people's lives. Enjoy the sense of fulfillment in the knowledge that you made a difference.

SKILLS TO GAIN AT THIS PHASE

At this stage, the most important skill to learn is *how to mentor* so you can better teach, advise, and guide. Numerous studies have found that mentoring, when done well, is a mutually beneficial reciprocal and collaborative relationship.[17] You'll benefit by mentoring others at this stage.

Imparting what you have done and how you have done it might be intuitive but there are some important skills to learn to be a successful mentor. We suggest the following:

1. Learn how to build trust with your mentee, usually through active listening, authentic conversations, and finding a shared professional interest. Mentoring is not a one-way, share-your-life-story

experience. Research has found that mentors with cognition-based trust and affect-based trust can offer the most successful outcomes for their mentees.[18] This means that you need to understand what is in your mentee's head and heart—and grow their trust through both your relational support and competent advice-giving.

2. Get to know your mentee as a person and develop a supportive relationship. The better the quality of your relationship with your mentee, the more likely your mentee will follow your advice.[19] Your mentee's motivations and natural talents are not the same as yours. Just because you made certain career decisions (and they worked for you), does not mean that the same choices will be right for your mentee. Appreciate what makes your mentee tick and the context in which they are trying to grow their career. While their journey might look different, you still have much to offer.

3. Be committed to the mentee's development by being strategic with the timing of introductions. This might mean determining the best time to engage your mentee with those in your network. The best time might be now—but it might be too soon: Sometimes mentors open too many doors too quickly and the mentee just isn't ready to walk through them successfully.

4. Be honest and provide constructive feedback. This is sometimes the most uncomfortable part about being a mentor—offering feedback that might bruise your mentee's ego but is critically important because it can derail your mentee's career if not heeded. Learn how to gently offer this advice after you have established trust.

5. Be authentic. When mentors only share the successes in their careers, they come off as inauthentic and bragging. Keep it real. We don't recommend wearing your Presidential Medal to your first meeting. Balance the description of your career wins with how you have handled the setbacks you encountered.

YOUR MINDSET AT THIS PHASE

At this stage your overarching mindset should be one of *effective altruism*. The effective altruism movement was given a spotlight when William MacAskill and his colleagues through the Centre for Effective Altruism[20] in England began to encourage people to more rationally consider where to volunteer their time, donate their money, and the like. They encourage everyone who is in a position to give back to do so using evidence and reason to figure out how to benefit others as much as possible.

Too often our choices for giving of time or money are generated by emotional response or convenience rather than rational decision-making. We'd like to see everyone apply this same logic when selecting their career acts in this give-back phase. Let's take the example of a person who has an enjoyable "helper's high" experience by picking up litter with friends for a few hours at the local park. That same person, using more career-oriented effective altruism, could have used the same few hours (along with her stellar financial skills and great communication style) to teach investing skills to high school students who just started their first summer jobs. Not that the clean-up isn't worthwhile, but given what we know about compound interest, most would agree that the latter experience would have a more positive impact for more people in the longer term.

To build your effective altruism for this career phase, we have adapted some excellent advice offered by the Centre for Effective Altruism:

- Use your time, talents, and money in situations that will have the greatest ability to influence the greatest numbers. As an example, when Andy provided the seed investment for Skiilify, the company Paula and Andy co-founded, he did so to democratize the critical soft skills that were not readily available to many without the resources of an elite university education. We set Skiilify up as a public benefit corporation to maintain this aspect of its mission.

- Focus on the situations that are highly neglected over those with the greatest levels of attention. For example, rather than mentoring your neighbor's affluent college student, could you offer the same time to a student with fewer resources and opportunities?

- Place your time, money, and talent into situations with the greatest likelihood that you can solve a problem. Ask more questions to see whether the situation is tractable. Solving a problem whether on a grand or small scale feels much more satisfying than feeling as though your time or money have been wasted.

The one message we want you to gain from this book is to take personal ownership of your career acts through **all the phases** of the journey. You have choices to make; time, money, and energy to allocate; and a life to live (and harmonize). It is your responsibility to create your own fulfilling career acts at each phase.

KEY TAKEAWAYS

- Be realistic about your current and necessary skill level to succeed in your ideal career acts. Use your starter and foundational career acts to gain those skills.

- Select your career acts carefully at each phase. The way you decide on a career act at one phase might be different from the way you decide on a career act at another phase. Babysitting for the neighbors is a great job in junior high, but not a high-wage option in your twenties. Be discerning by focusing on the goals for that specific phase of your career.

- Understand the way in which your mindset might need to shift as you move through the phases of your career, maximizing your expectations. At an earlier phase you should maximize development and growth, while at a later phase you should maximize time and influence.

- Invest in yourself by developing your skills at every phase of your career. The greater the skills you possess, the more control you will have over your career and the faster you will move to the next phase.

- Regardless of where you are on your career journey, give yourself a license to try new career acts that look interesting. Your interests might change over time.

- You can have multiple concurrent career paths, each at different phases. It is OK to simultaneously be at the beginning of one career path while at a later stage of another.

- The best careers will always require you to take some risks or make some investments in yourself.

CHAPTER 5

CONSIDER SIMULTANEOUS CAREER ACTS

I don't think much of a man who is not wiser today than he was yesterday.
—ABRAHAM LINCOLN

Peter Shankman wears his heart (and his professional mission) on his sleeve, metaphorically speaking. And he's turned his personal mission into a series of simultaneous and successful career acts. His web page sums up his mission well, saying: "How can I help you?" It bears the logos of leading companies that he's helped over the years as a master communicator and connector. It also offers tons of free advice (as well as for-pay tools) about being an effective and heartfelt communicator in our complex, increasingly online world.

Not bad for someone with attention-deficit/hyperactive disorder (ADHD).

Born in New York City, Peter came of age in the early days of the commercial Internet. An only child and the son of music professors, he graduated from NYC's famous Fiorello H. LaGuardia High School of Music & Art and Performing Arts and then Boston University, where he majored in communications. Post-grad, he was attending Brooks Institute of Photography in Southern California for fashion and commercial photography, when his financial aid dried up. With eighteen credits to go, he lost his financial aid and had to leave graduate school.

Back in NYC and unemployed, he was in a chat room on the America Online network and learned he could post his résumé for a job in the AOL newsroom. Despite his lack of work experience, he was hired. Moving to Virginia, he became one of the founding news editors at AOL, helping establish the AOL Newsroom.[1] After three great years there, he left AOL and headed back to NYC, where he briefly consulted and tried a career in print journalism (soon to learn that it was not for him; too structured).

In 1998, he started a public relations firm, the Geek Factory, to help clients benefiting from the commercialization of the Internet. Launched from his NYC apartment "with one cat and one computer," it very quickly became successful and eventually helped clients beyond just PR. The Geek Factory was acquired by a larger firm in 2001 (while continuing to operate under its original name and with its original staff).[2]

Naturally gregarious and now with a huge Rolodex (i.e., professional connections, for those under forty-five) of both business colleagues and press contacts, Peter had started helping journalists with sources for their stories as a friendly gesture. Help A Reporter Out (HARO) was thus born in 2008, eventually growing into a popular, ad-supported service that enabled journalists to get feedback from the public. HARO fundamentally changed the way that storytellers of all kinds connected with sources in the age of the web and social media. The service, which he eventually spun off as its own business, was acquired by Vocus, the PR marketing software firm (now Cision) in 2010. HARO remains a staple for modern professional communicators today.

Along the way, Peter has written several books related to his craft and his passion: connecting companies, customers, and people. He is also the author of *Faster Than Normal: Turbocharge Your Focus, Productivity, and Success with the Secrets of the ADHD Brain.* The 2017 book "rewrites the script on ADHD," detailing his personal journey with ADHD (he was diagnosed as an adult) and how he has learned not only how to live with ADHD but also turned it into a positive attribute in his career. More recently, he published *The Boy with the Faster Brain*, a book for children with ADHD and their parents. Endowed with a disability ("a gift") that he turned into an ability, Peter Shankman is an excellent example of how to build and optimize simultaneous career acts based on doing what you love. (Even if you never do it quite at his pace or scale.)

Beyond being a valued advisor and consultant to companies, he's become a much-sought-after public speaker. Peter regularly talks about his experience with ADHD while delivering marketing-related lectures and talks about channeling it for one's own benefits. People (anyone!) can engage with Peter on his blog, his podcast (about ADHD), his listserv or on LinkedIn. In addition, he's invested his energy, expertise, and enthusiasm as an angel investor in start-up companies and as an advisor and board member to others.

Some people might perceive Peter's career as lacking focus, an overt indication of his ADHD. We see the opposite, perceiving Peter's career to be an ideal approach, both strategic and laudable—an approach we encourage you to model. (Score one for neural diversity and the inclination toward adult ADHD!)

Just like the diversification mentality you use with your financial portfolio; we encourage you to use your talents to diversify your sources of income in multiple, simultaneous career acts. As with an investment portfolio, bad things can happen when you place all your money in one stock. *(Are you old enough to remember Enron?)* Each career act should be an independent source of income and fulfilling from the perspective of growth, development, and engagement with your talents.

We have seen examples of simultaneous career acts all around us:

- The actor Jessica Alba started a company, Honest, focusing on natural, eco-friendly products for babies, personal care, cosmetics, and cleaning.

- The professional basketball player for the Denver Nuggets, Tyler Lydon, also ran a summer basketball camp for children in conjunction with Nike.

- The country music singer Blake Shelton has a successful recording career, has been a judge on every season of the TV show The Voice, and owns a restaurant chain called Ole Red.

If none of these people were recognizable, *how about Benjamin Franklin?* Franklin is one of America's first and most famous examples of successful multiple career acts as a scientist, inventor, politician, and publisher, among other laudable credentials.

You don't need to be rich, famous, or a founding father of a country to have multiple, simultaneous career acts. They are within reach of anyone who has in-demand technical skills, great execution on their innovative ideas, and energy. They are colleagues and friends of yours who are using their talents for either *related* or *unrelated* career acts.

People with related career acts are generally able to use a personal or professional "brand" to propel their reputation within a field. Here are some examples:

- A physical therapist with a private practice, who also works part-time for a minor-league baseball team

- A middle-school English teacher who offers English as a Second Language classes to new immigrants in the evenings

- A retail women's clothing store manager who started an online consignment store

- A mechanic who works for an auto shop and rebuilds mid-1960s Corvettes for resale

- A Pilates instructor who is employed by a national gym chain, but is also a virtual personal trainer on her own time

Other individuals have multiple career acts that form a *personal coherence*. In these cases, while their career acts might not be in the same area, their skills from one career act often help to differentiate them in another career act. See if you can connect the dots for the following examples:

- A part-time cardiac nurse who runs an organic catering business for wellness-oriented clients

- An electrical engineer who publishes science fiction novels with a technology theme

- A project manager for a software company who owns and manages six rental properties

- A corporate accountant who started an online service to tutor high school students in math

- A maître d' of a high-end restaurant who started a matchmaking service

Whether in fields that are directly related or just personally coherent, many people today have thriving and fulfilling simultaneous career acts. Research[3] found that one of the primary motivations for holding multiple positions concurrently is career advancement, whether to develop competencies, learn new skills, leverage existing skills, or network. The study found that synergies between career acts are individually determined based on how people are motivated to shape their careers. In other words, if this is the career journey you want, you should choose the course that makes sense for the skills you want to grow and use. You have the power to program the coordinates for your career journey into your own personal career GPS (and you can keep updating the software).

In this chapter, we want you to discern for yourself whether a multiple, simultaneous career act approach is right for you. Spoiler alert: This type of a career is not right for everyone. If at some point during this chapter you decide that multiple career acts are not how you roll, then you will appreciate the next chapter. Until then, keep an open mind and explore:

- The mindset needed to enjoy a career with multiple career acts
- A diagnostic for multiple career acts to increase both satisfaction and income
- The selection of multiple career acts to ensure you are moving toward your ideal career
- The challenge of multiple career acts in different career stages
- The ethical considerations for multiple career acts

Mindset for multiple career acts

Do you have the right mentality to engage in multiple career acts? The answer might be that, for you, one solid career act at a time is the best one for you. No judgment here either way. We are just presenting options and ways to diagnose what will work best for your ideal career.

Before we jump into the diagnostic, we want to prime you with some self-awareness. People with multiple career acts call them by different names, like a "new gig" or a "side hustle." *How do you react when you hear that a friend has a new talent-related side hustle?* Is the reaction, "I knew they spent too much on that last trip to South Beach" or is it "I am so glad they are finally starting what they have wanted to do." The difference should be revealing—do you see your friend's extra roles as a positive or a negative feature in their career?

Try another primer, this time thinking about a couple:

Bobby and Tess. Tess is a nanny during the day and loves to engage in her hobby of photography in the evenings and on weekends. Exciting for Tess, her evening and weekend fun has become increasingly profitable, so she has been gradually cutting back her hours as a nanny. Bobby, her husband, is an IT professional by day. As a second career act, Bobby is a web designer under retainer, keeping the clients' pages current, interactive, and engaging. He also designs web pages for solopreneurs, including one for his wife's photography business. Happy with the way their careers are growing, the couple also reached a personal milestone when they bought their first house.

Do you think that Tess and Bobby are stretched thin because they are doing too much or fulfilled because they are following their professional hearts? Bobby and Tess will admit that their co-created personal and professional lives are not always easy to harmonize. They knew they were serious about this when they decided to sync their calendars. They are busy. They couldn't tell you what is happening in the latest reality TV show, and they need to schedule just about everything in their lives, including date nights and related activities that otherwise happen with greater spontaneity.

The question for the purpose of this diagnostic is whether you think Bobby and Tess are happy (or unhappy) individually and as a couple. *Do you think they are supporting each other as they move closer to their ideal portfolio careers—or just two people distracted with what they are doing independently?* Your opinion of Tess and Bobby will reveal your attitudes about simultaneous career acts.

The idea of multiple career acts might seem daunting at first. Chances are high, however, that you are already balancing multiple roles in your life (e.g., student, parent, employee, volunteer, caregiver, coach). This idea of having multiple roles in your life isn't such a huge departure from what most people already do; the idea is just being applied to your career. *How do you view the multiple roles in your life?*

LIVE FOR A LIVING

OK, you have explored a few primers, now it is time for the diagnostic. To what extent do you agree with the following statements:

1. I believe that people who have side hustles are only doing it for the money.

2. Most people with multiple gigs or roles are having financial problems and trying to make ends meet.

3. The only people who can successfully have multiple sources of income without stress are those who have personal wealth.

4. It is better to do one job well than to try to have multiple roles.

5. I would never have the time or energy to work on more than one role.

How did you score? The more you agree with the previous statements, the less likely you are to want to have multiple, simultaneous career acts. Even so, we encourage you to keep reading for a nugget or two on portfolio careers. We want you to expand what is possible—but do it in a way that remains true to your values. The only way to create your ideal career is to be honest with yourself. The more you disagree with the previous statements, the more likely you are to thrive with multiple, simultaneous career acts. With this mindset, keep reading. This approach will be helpful to build your ideal career.

Everyone will be different in their acceptance of multiple, simultaneous career acts; this includes your family and friends. If you have a mindset that supports simultaneous career acts, we need to offer fair warning that there are likely to be naysayers in your life, those who want you to have a more conventional career. Under the old rules of employment, people with multiple career acts would be chastised by parents, a spouse, or a nosy mother-in-law for "not having a professional focus," "not being serious about your job," "not sticking with it," and "being too distracted." If you have the right mindset for multiple career acts, just give them your best teenage-inspired eye roll and keep doing what you are doing. (Scratch that. Be diplomatic with your mother-in-law and skip the eye roll.)

We would not be doing our job if we were idealistic about this approach to managing your own career. Usually, when people engage in multiple career acts, especially at the start, they are working when others are not. It is described as the difference between what you do from 9am to 5pm and weekdays (career act #1) and what you do from 5 to 9pm and weekends (career act #2, #3, etc.). If you don't have a career journey that will motivate you to work while your family and friends are relaxing and not working, then you might want to build a greater level of self-awareness before jumping in. Time is a precious and limited commodity. Use it wisely to have fewer regrets.

Dan Pink and a research team launched the World Regret Survey, analyzing the reason for individuals' regrets across multiple life domains, such as work, family, education.[4] The study found that one of the four categories of regrets was "boldness regrets"—regretting what you did not try or the chances you did not take. He wrote, "What haunts us is the inaction itself. Foregone opportunities to leave our hometown or launch a business or chase a true love or see the world all linger in the same way."

Sometimes people who want to try an additional career act will resist because they feel they will be cognitively stretched thin. Research[5] found just the opposite to be true: the empowerment felt from a desirable second part-time career act *enhanced* full-time work performance. People with a motivating and engaging second career act were less likely to have it conflict—and even more likely to have it enrich—their performance in their primary job. It is the same way a great side dish won't conflict—and likely will enrich—the main course.

If simultaneous career acts comprise the career journey that would be right for you, we want to provide some direction and help you see this as an option. If the thought of emphasizing the work domain of your life doesn't appeal to you, then we want to help you find a career journey that aligns with your life goals. *This is your journey.*

Diagnosis for multiple career acts

Since our twenties, both of us have had multiple career acts. We like what we do and identified various ways to configure and reconfigure our talents to create multiple (and very different) opportunities that placed us into states of flow. For each new role, we followed the approach for stages (from the previous chapter) resulting in a career at any given time with roles in various stages.

For Andy, his early interest in programming and technology, coupled with his short attention span and competitive streak (from playing rugby), jump-started a first career act in helping launch and grow tech start-ups (Trilogy, pcOrder.com, Bowstreet). He later realized that he had built a lot of software, sold a lot of software, and made a bunch of money, but felt as though he needed to have a broader social impact in the next phase of his career. He was encouraged by his mentors Frank Moss and Steve Holtzman to focus on *delivering better software, systems, and data to scientists and doctors working to discover drugs that improve human health*. From that insight, Andy helped start Infinity Pharmaceuticals—a spinout of chemistry from Harvard University—and eventually took a role running data and software engineering at the Novartis Institutes for BioMedical Research. While Andy was at Novartis, he wanted to stay connected to the start-up community, so he started a seed fund called Koa Labs. The fund was just his money and was focused on backing first-time entrepreneurs who come from traditionally underserved communities.

Paula fell in love with the research process as an undergraduate student, enjoying the creative energy of knowledge creation and the development of individual assessments based on her research. Early in her career (after graduate school and while still in her twenties), she was drawn to keynote speaking and consulting—in addition to her academic position as a faculty member at the university. These became career acts for her, rooted in what she loves to do.

All great career acts are as diverse as the people who occupy them. Career acts are often combined and reconfigured throughout our careers to achieve ever-increasing career satisfaction.

Terrific. Thanks. But "how the heck do *I* start?" you might be asking.

1. To begin this process, we want you to think of your current primary job (or the one you seek) as career act #1.

2. Next, do you have any other income-creating activities in which you engage? These can be activities such as running an Etsy business, driving for a ride-share, working a weekend landscaping job, tutoring, freelance graphic design, giving guitar lessons for thirteen-year-old budding rock stars, or selling your paintings at the local art festival. If you have any income-producing activities outside your primary career act, those are your additional career acts (#2, #3, #4, etc.).

3. Now, think about these career acts as you complete the following exercise.

Exercise: Your current career acts

What are your current career acts?

Career act #1 _____

Career act #2 _____

Career act #3 _____

Career act #4 _____

On a scale from 1% to 100%, how fulfilling or satisfying is each career act? If the career act is 100% satisfying, you would say "I am so giddy doing this, I would pay someone to let me continue." If you find a career act 90% satisfying you might say, "I feel fortunate to be paid for what I love doing." And so goes the slide down to 5% satisfying where you might utter "there is no amount of money that would keep me doing this for much longer."

Career act #1 _____ % satisfying

Career act #2 _____ % satisfying

Career act #3 _____ % satisfying

Career act #4 _____ % satisfying

Adding all lines to 100%, what percentage of your total annual income is derived from each career act?

Career act #1 _____ % of my total income

Career act #2 _____ % of my total income

Career act #3 _____ % of my total income

Career act #4 _____ % of my total income

If you are like most people, only the line for career act #1 is filled and it is only 10% to 50% satisfying—but it accounts for 100% of your total income.

If you have additional interesting career acts that are between 75% to 90% satisfying, they are likely to account for less than 10% of your total income. If you have additional dissatisfying career acts, you might be doing them to make ends meet. We get it and have been there. Most people find that their career act #1 provides income while the additional career acts provide more satisfaction or supplemental income.

This diagnostic is the starting point, but likely far from your ideal career situation. If multiple, simultaneous career acts are desirable for you, we want you to derive a better return on the effort in terms of both income and satisfaction for each career act in which you engage. Your goal will be to derive more satisfaction from each career act or have one great career act that provides both the income you want and the satisfaction you seek. Over time, as you develop your career acts, you will begin to see these indicators shift. As these shift, most people find that their careers become more stimulating, balanced, and secure.

Having *necessity-based* multiple career acts is different from *purposeful* multiple career acts. When your multiple career acts are necessity-based, one or more career acts are temporary while (hopefully) providing resources for your career journey. These necessity-based career acts keep your refrigerator stocked and the lights on. These sources of income might be temporary or seasonal jobs, a flexible gig (e.g., Uber, Task Rabbit), a project-based assignment, or a part-time position in an unrelated field. Aspiring actors who have waited tables while taking acting lessons or college students working part-time jobs unrelated to their careers have experienced this. If you are in this situation, we hope you can generate income (and hopefully some benefits) that will help you start your career journey. While not the enduring way to have multiple career acts, there might be hidden advantages to necessity-based career acts. For example, a friend who waited tables at a diner while working on a degree in writing, wrote her first novel about a waitress at a diner.

Purposeful multiple career acts are different. This is a way of managing your career overall. Most often (but not always), people who engage in this type of career are past the foundational stages and want to diversify their career portfolio.

Selection of multiple career acts

In this portfolio-style, diversification approach to your career journey, the same is true. Each career act will have its own trajectory. Unfortunately, this is where most people get it wrong. They start pursuing additional career acts out of boredom or because they are "flattered to be asked." Both reasons are the carbon monoxide of career management; you'll pursue them, oblivious to their detrimental consequences to your career. They will drain your time and stall you, without moving you forward.

Being recognized for our accomplishments feels great. This is true for us. It is true for you. It is true for everyone. It is gratifying to be asked to teach a course, join a board, consult, tutor, or do whatever because we are great at what we are doing. We want you to enjoy this recognition. Bask in the warm glow of flattery for a day or two. Appreciate being asked. Then (possibly), decline the offer.

We want you to ignore these siren calls **unless the opportunity is a desirable step in your career journey.** If you accept an additional career act out of boredom, you have waited passively for something to come to you—which might not align with where you hope to go. If all one needs to do is flatter you to take you off your career journey, then you've just relinquished control again—only this time to your self-esteem. Stay in control. Use recognition and the new opportunities coming your way as a great sign: you are being recognized for your knowledge, skills, and abilities. Once you've read the email from a university colleague inviting you to teach a course in a subject that won't help your career, forward a copy to your family to make them happy to call you "professor" for a few hours. Then respond to your university colleague by politely declining the offer and maybe offer to guest lecture for an hour.

Staying in the driver's seat, you can now decide whether an opportunity (or which opportunity) will move you closer to your ideal career. Here are three questions to help you decide if the additional career act is right for you:

1. *Is this an opportunity that would help you <u>leverage your existing competencies</u> in an industry or area that is new to you?* This is a potentially ideal opportunity for you if your career act #1 is developmental but not in the field or industry you want longer term. This possible opportunity should be considered if it will expose you to a network of people who are aligned with your ideal career or enables you to use your competencies within a field or industry of interest. Andy took what might have looked like a veering left-hand turn to friends and family when he took that administrative role in a biotechnology start-up. But it got him into the industry. From that context, he got an invaluable education in the industry in a short amount of time.

The team was incredible and collaborative, and many remain valued colleagues to this day. For Andy, the inspirational founder and CEO of that start-up became a role model, a lasting friend, and mentor to him, as a future founder of companies. With the help of mentors, Andy leveraged his technology and operational knowledge to immerse himself in a new field and industry that provided incredible intellectual stimulation.

2. *Is this an opportunity that would help you <u>develop or enhance your existing competencies</u>?* This is a potentially ideal opportunity if your career act #1 is aligned with your ideal industry, has you on the career journey you desire, but not stretching you (fast) enough to elevate your competencies. In this situation, your organization recognizes that you are great at what you do and is leveraging you *in place.* Own your professional development with career act #2 that will stretch and build your critical competencies.

3. *Is this an opportunity that would help you <u>gain new competencies</u>?* A second career act might be an ideal opportunity if your career act #1 is aligned with your ideal industry but lacks any opportunity to build the competencies you need for your ideal career. Paula viewed her ideal career in making academic research accessible to those who need it across a variety of channels (Skiilify, books, podcasts, TV). She had been a university professor for almost twenty years when she started doing a regular segment called "Reclaim Your Career" for CNN. Translating research and advising in two-to-three-minute segments on camera was a new skill she wanted to learn. (She is still learning that one.)

At this point, you have a better sense of your mindset on developing your career. If you are still interested in managing your career the way you would manage a financial portfolio, with multiple simultaneous career acts, please keep reading. If that sounds chaotic, stressful, or not your ideal career goal, move ahead to the next chapter. We'll catch up.

The stages of multiple career acts

OK, you are still with us. This means that you are still flirting with the possibility of a career that includes multiple career acts. The first few chapters discussed how to select and grow your ideal career. What about growing the other career acts? No surprise here: The same rules apply. The process for building your second and third career act is the same as it is to engage in just one. The big difference is that growth for each career act will not likely happen evenly. You might be very advanced in one career act but at the most entry-level stage in another.

Both of us have multiple career acts and have had a diversified career portfolio for much of our careers. We, like many who hold multiple career acts, have each of our career acts residing in very different phases. For Andy, his role as CEO for Tamr puts him in a high-growth phase. At the same time, his private equity organization, Koa Labs, puts him in the giving-back phase because he is investing in and mentoring budding entrepreneurs. As an author, Andy is in the foundational phase as this is his first book. For Paula, her academic career is in the giving-back phase with her most fulfilling activities embedded in mentoring and advising junior scholars and students. At the same time, she is in an early foundational phase as an entrepreneur, still learning, as she builds Skiilify, a company that we co-founded. (Thankfully, Andy has been an excellent mentor.)

Having career acts in different phases requires more than effective time management. Being at different levels across multiple career acts requires you to have the ability to mentally shift from how you are treated in your more advanced role (with esteem, admiration, competence) to how you are treated as a newbie in a different role. Research[6] looked at these status inconsistencies between full-time employment and other concurrent roles (i.e., second career acts in our parlance) and found that for those who had multiple jobs with inconsistent status were more likely to experience conflict about their sense of self. This is a mental version of flying first class in one direction and then having a middle seat, in the back of the plane near the restroom in economy class, on the return. Your brain is telling itself: *Wait. Don't they know who I am?* Paula has watched this unfold when senior leaders start adjunct teaching at the university. They are accustomed to greater administrative support and position power than is afforded to faculty.

We all want to be treated as we believe we should be treated. For this reason, it is important to mentally prepare for (and possibly embrace) the status shift. We appreciate egalitarianism, but you need to be prepared that you will likely be treated differently at different phases and have access to different resources commensurate with your career act's phase. If you cannot be comfortable and embrace the humility needed, multiple simultaneous career acts might not be right for you. If you have the confidence and self-esteem to engage in a lower phase career act with humility, this might be an effective approach for your career management.

The ethics of multiple career acts

Many people add career acts based on something they have been doing professionally, an extension of their current role, perhaps with another organization. This is common and logical because a current employment situation might have helped you increase your level of expertise and skills. We need to discuss the ethics of the noncompetition among your career acts—especially if your primary career act is working for an organization.

Here are five rules for adding career acts ethically:

1. **Avoid conflicts of interest.** Career acts should be, ideally, separate industries so you are not tempted to (or unintentionally) compete with your current employer, independent contracting, or freelancing activities. If your career acts are in the same industry, try the "newspaper test": If your career acts were on the front page of the newspaper, would you be embarrassed or fired for the activity?

2. **Do not borrow time, knowledge, or materials.** If it feels as though you are overstepping your bounds "borrowing" from one employer or client site to build a different career act, you probably are. This might be as seemingly innocuous as checking email for one career act while billing or being paid by another or it might be as unethical as working for another career act while being paid by your employer. Do not do this—do not even use a paper clip or envelope that has been in the supply closet for so long they are yellowing. Try the "manager or client test": Would you be comfortable telling your manager or client about your activity without any concern? When in doubt, open the dialogue with your manager or boss. Again, you shouldn't feel like you are cheating on your employer. Rather, you are managing your income and growing your career purposefully.

3. **Be sure you are not violating your contract.** If you work for one employer or if you signed a contract as an independent contractor or freelancer, your career acts might be limited (usually with non-compete clauses). Even if you did not sign a contract when you began working, you should check in your organization's policy manual or, more difficult to learn, the expected implicit norms of the organization.

4. **Report income honestly.** If you work for an employer in the United States, you will receive a W-2 form, including your income and some deductions, such as federal and state taxes and Social Security. If you work as an independent contractor, you should receive a 1099 form from each of your clients throughout the year. If you do not receive a 1099 from a given client or organization you should keep a record of income earned and expenses to accurately report your income for tax purposes (e.g., if you receive less than $600 from an organization, they do not need to generate

a 1099 for you but you will still need to report the income). As an aside, if you do much work outside of traditional employment settings, we also suggest you speak with a tax professional to be sure you are filing appropriately and receiving all the possible tax deductions.

5. **Do not poach clients—ever.** If you freelance and are employed in the same area where clients would be identical, you might experience a conflict of interest, which could be perceived as poaching clients. As before, try the "manager or client test": Would you be comfortable telling your manager about your conversations or work with clients without any concern that he or she would view them as a conflict of interest?

It is worth repeating (again and again), we want you to take personal ownership of your career goals and the journey along the way. You have choices to make; time, money, and energy to allocate; and a life to live (and harmonize). No employer, no boss or mentor, no professor or teacher, no parent, partner, or spouse—no one—will be able to create the career journey that is right for you; it is your responsibility to create your own fulfilling career. Love it or dread it—it's yours. We want you to love it. And, if that includes having multiple sources of income because that is what you want, then we say, "go for it!" We did and enjoyed it. We also know that it is not right for everyone.

We do not advocate working longer hours or toiling in multiple jobs. Multiple dull career acts would only result in a very dull (and even more stressful) life. We also do not advocate running yourself ragged trying to do multiple jobs (even if they are engaging). We advocate finding multiple income-creating activities that you sincerely enjoy, that fit with your life in a fulfilling, harmonized way, and that offer you financial freedom because you are not relying on any one employment setting. This isn't about luck or time. It is about smart progression for each career act.

KEY TAKEAWAYS

- Having multiple simultaneous career acts is not the right approach for everyone. You'll need the right mindset to want to have multiple roles.

- Multiple career acts require you to (often) work while your loved ones are not. Think through whether this is right for you.

- Do not accept a second career act out of either flattery or boredom. While such second career acts seem right in the moment, they are not where you should invest your time—unless they are aligned with your career journey.

- If a second career act will help you develop or gain competencies you need for an ideal career or give you the exposure to the industry of your ideal career, the opportunity might be a valuable investment.

- Each career act grows in its own stage. This will require humility to be more senior in one career act and possibly more junior in another.

- If you decide to add career acts, do so ethically.

CHAPTER 6

BE INDISPENSABLE

Don't make money your goal. Instead, pursue the things you love doing,
and then do them so well that people can't take their eyes off you.
—MAYA ANGELOU

Born and raised in a small town in Maine, Michelle Kydd Lee was a young
woman looking for a life of adventure and a way to help other people, a
family value and foundation of her upbringing.[1] Michelle's boldness—a trait
since she was a baby—coupled with deaths of close friends framed her entrepreneurial approach to her career.

In her early twenties, Michelle packed up her old Volkswagen Jetta,
headed west, and landed a job in Southern California with a nonprofit community organization. Through an almost Hollywood-esque meeting in a
diner, she met an agent who weeks later would become president of CAA,
the creative-talent powerhouse in the entertainment industry. She shared her
work enthusiasm and dreams with him at lunch, and he offered her a job.

At age twenty-nine, Michelle established the pioneering CAA Foundation, which deploys the firm's social responsibility as a shaper of
popular culture to do good work that benefits society. Over the next
twenty-five years, Michelle grew from a traditional nonprofit person into

a businessperson and practicing "intrapreneur." She took on more people, challenges, and divisional management roles, eventually becoming the first woman named to the board and the management committee. Today, she's CAA's Chief Innovation Officer, having trained and handed off the foundation to "incredible people who are the next generation's version of what I did when I was twenty-nine."

Along the way, Michelle has mentored dozens of people. She's advanced and publicly shared management philosophies about finding, cultivating, and promoting the best talent from all walks of life. As a senior manager and board member at CAA, she's strived to level the playing field for talent and create a more equitable world. For example: the pioneering CAA Elevate program provides a learning track for young people to become talent agents, giving many others a shot at this coveted career.

As a senior officer in a high-profile company, Michelle has this message for today's employers. "Today, employers have to be curious about the lives of their employees," she says. "For example, are they struggling with college debt, as many are? That might dictate the job path that they take as it's essential to get a foothold on finances as quickly as possible to make the right decisions going forward. For those not struggling with college debt, that's a privilege and one should recognize it as such. But employers—not employees—need to set up an equitable environment."

"Whatever ZIP code you were born into or whatever family you were born into, that doesn't mean that that's where the talent lies," she says. "But traditionally, that's how talent has been mined. If we flip that and say talent is everywhere, how do we find great talent, create a safe space for them to grow and thrive? All society will benefit."

Michelle's career acts, all within a single company, have been highly self-directed, non-incremental, and (most importantly) purpose- and interest-driven. By defining her relationship with her career early on, she achieved her dream. "My personal outlook on life continues to be this: make sure I'm open when the universe presents an opportunity. Don't be so afraid of change or what could be. Capitalize on that moment with gusto. When opportunity knocks, let it in."

Like Michelle, it is possible your career path might take you on a journey with a single employer provided you follow her advice to own your future, stretch into opportunities, and live your purpose.

Careers like Michelle's with a single employer are less common than they were in decades past. However, working for a single employer for a substantial portion of your career might be a great approach for you, provided you remain in control as Michelle did. This single-employer approach has some advantages if it fits with the journey toward your ideal career. Working for a single employer for many years gives you a deep understanding of the context; better than an outsider, you will be able to navigate the organizational culture, internal politics, and expectations for advancement. You understand the terrain, seeing both the tripwires and opportunities that the newcomers might miss.

Once believed to be the safest way to manage a career, long tenure with a single employer today is a very risky strategy. In addition to all the reasons discussed in previous chapters, knowing the context as it is today does not mean it won't change. Downsizings. Mergers. Acquisitions. Reorganizations. These could disrupt what you thought was certain, making your understanding of your employer relatively useless. Ask anyone who once worked for Kodak, Enron, or Lehman Brothers. Things can change fast, not for the better.

If you want long tenure with a single employer, we want you to create a metaphorical safety net. Your safety net will be a function of how critical and unique you are to your employer, team, clients, and any others who make decisions about your continued employment.

To create a visual for this chapter, think for a minute about Karl Wallenda, the founder and leader of the famous daredevil family of stunt performers known as "The Flying Wallendas." Wallenda was once quoted as saying that "life is being on the wire, everything else is just waiting." During a high-wire act in 1978, Karl Wallenda fell to his death at age seventy-three. He died, as many have said, doing what he loved.[2] Nonetheless, Wallenda—as everyone—would benefit from a career with a safety net.

If you aspire to a career with a single employer, we want you to **create a career safety net**. The career safety net is created by becoming *indispensable*, like Michelle. Lofty, we know, but being an indispensable employee is attainable if you know the recipe. This chapter provides each of the five ingredients, the goals you should strive to achieve in every role:

1. Criticality

2. Uniqueness

3. Reliability

4. Visibility

5. Excellence

VISIT MYJOURNII.COM

Complete the Assessment to Understand Your CURVE

If you occupy (or want to occupy) a single career act, we strongly encourage you to take some time to work through this exercise for your current job. (You can also use that assessment to diagnose what might have gone wrong at an organization you left in the past.)

When you assess your CURVE, you'll better understand your job's safety net. Remember, CURVE stands for:

1. Criticality

2. Uniqueness

3. Reliability

4. Visibility

5. Excellence

To better remember this five-ingredient recipe to create a career safety net, we have a useful mnemonic device: the word "CURVE"—as in seeing around the curve or staying ahead of the curve. This chapter shares a bit more about each ingredient—and all the garnishes to make yourself indispensable in every role.

Criticality: Occupy an essential role in the organization

If you are in a support-staff or ancillary role in your organization, you are in the riskiest possible position because you are one of the first to be downsized when organizational cuts are needed. Most organizations manage their human resources well enough to know that the last people they would ever cut in an economic downturn would be those in wealth-creating positions. Employees who are creating high-demand products and services—and those who are effectively selling them—are the most secure.

Professional employees and senior executives are not immune from being downsized. As Drs. Mark Huselid, Dick Beatty, and Brian Becker note in their seminal books and articles, the critical "A" positions are those crucial to a company's ability to execute some part of the company's strategy.[3]

Are you in one of those critical roles? Criticality to the organization is not about the level in the organization. Even well-qualified professionals are encouraged to think carefully about the type of role they select for their career acts. For example, a lawyer who is a member of a manufacturing company's legal department would be in a support role (i.e., he or she costs or saves the company money). This job's safety net might resemble a basketball hoop with large holes at the top and the bottom. The same lawyer working for a law firm would be in a wealth-creating role (i.e., he or she brings in money for the company). This job's safety net is big, strong, and well-supported. When possible, try to align your career moves to offer your critical talents with the way your employer creates wealth. Your success will be central to the success of your employer.

Uniqueness: Have skills that are difficult to replace in the job market

In the eyes of those who love us, we are all irreplaceable. Unfortunately, in terms of the education, experience, knowledge, skills, and abilities we bring to our employers, some of us are considered more unique than others. If your position is one that could be accomplished by many individuals effectively, you are less unique than someone who is succeeding in a role that very few people could accomplish effectively. Consider your role in the organization: *Are there others who do your job?* Consider the labor market: *How difficult would it be to find your replacement?* Be honest with yourself. Across your career acts you want to demonstrate your unique skills, ideally performing each of your career acts in a way that would be almost impossible for your employer to replace.

Try to attain roles that will leverage your unique knowledge, skills, and abilities (and ideally your talents, passions, and interests also). If you do not have a unique set of knowledge, skills, and abilities, consider the way you do your job: *Are there ways you can accomplish your job that brings additional value to the role, but leverages something only you could do in the way you accomplish your job?* Being the only bilingual customer service person in an area that needs your language skills or being a corporate trainer who can make even the dullest material entertaining and engaging are two examples of ways to highlight your uniqueness.

Reliability: Under-promise and over-deliver

Are you the "go-to" person in your work group when things need to be accomplished on a tight deadline or the work is particularly critical? You are already considered a reliable performer. If you aren't sure and need a diagnostic along with some advice on how to become someone who is highly reliable, try these:

Don't complain. Last-minute requests, short deadlines, and other pressured work situations are a part of everyone's job from time to time. How you handle these requests will speak volumes about your reliability. We encourage you to handle challenging requests with grace. That said, we don't want you to be a doormat. If chaotic requests become unreasonable, we encourage you to use diplomacy and set some boundaries with your boss. Ask for "clarity around priorities" so you can continue to do your job well, aligned with the changing demands. People respect boundaries.

Be available. This does not mean that you should always be the first one in the office every morning and the last one to leave every evening. In fact, in most organizational cultures, this just demonstrates your inefficiency. Rather, if additional work is needed due to a particularly challenging time, an unexpected project, filling in for a colleague who is sick, etc., be available and willing to help. If an encroachment on your life becomes the norm, diplomatically ask for role clarity. It helps to know exactly what tasks you would like to shed and which ones you want to continue when you have this conversation.

Offer more value than what is requested. Try to anticipate what else would be useful and if you can provide it effectively, do it. For example, if you are asked to put together a presentation based on some materials, also put together the corresponding speaker's notes, the notes the speaker can use to give his or her presentation. The first time a research assistant did that for Paula, she quickly became Paula's indispensable "go-to" person. Some work environments offer more opportunities to show your value in different ways. Andy has had incredible experiences with work environments where there were few boundaries put on people's ambition. At Trilogy in Austin, Texas, founder Joe Liemandt was known for encouraging young people to take risks and do whatever it took to exceed expectations. Andy was inspired by this culture of "the only bottleneck to your success is you." Some people were overwhelmed but Andy found it liberating as there were infinite opportunities to over-perform and do things that other people thought impossible.

Deliver on promises. "Under-promise and over-deliver" is a popular quote by business guru Tom Peters. We appreciate this quote and share it frequently with those we mentor to help our mentees positively shape their reputations. Overpromising (even with the best of intentions) unfortunately damages professional reputations when you fail to deliver, negatively affecting your credibility and the perceptions of your competence. Guaranteeing that you can build a new app for your company by Friday when you've never coded might not be a good idea. It is always better to consistently exceed everyone's expectations. Promising that you can put a team together to deliver the app in beta form by next quarter might be smarter. (Remember that accolades are not often given for merely meeting expectations, only exceeding them.) Try to balance the following three factors the next time you make a promise on a work-related deliverable:

1. Promises on work products: It is always a good idea to over-deliver on the quality of your work product by giving your client, supervisor, or colleague more than what they are expecting. Unless there is some perverse professional jealously, over-delivering on the quality of your work will help build trust and reflect positively on your credibility and competence.

2. Promises on deadlines: With respect to deadlines, producing something well ahead of schedule can sometimes be interpreted negatively—as if you are not expending the appropriate level of effort on the work product. Promise and adhere to the most realistic deadline possible. Deliver when you say you will deliver, unless delivering early would be preferred and you have already achieved excellence. If you are finished ahead of time, use the time to improve the quality of the work product.

3. Promises on resources: Managing your promises on budget or other necessary resources needed for a work product is nuanced. If you come in under expectations, you might be appreciated

temporarily (provided the quality is high); however, in doing so you have permanently set your resource expectation for future projects! In most circumstances, it is better to accurately estimate the time, money, staff, or whatever resources are needed and use the resources in a way that is consistent with those expectations. The positive benefit of coming in under budget or using fewer resources is never as great as you would expect because the resources were already committed. "Wow," a supervisor might think, "She built an entire prototype for under one thousand dollars! From now on, we're slashing our prototype budgets!" They are "sunk costs" so already spent in the minds of those allocating the resource. The opposite might be more damaging: asking for more resources part of the way through the project. It gives the sense (whether deserved or not) of being unable to manage your resources effectively.

Deciding what to promise and when to deliver is an art in the professional world and important for protecting your reputation as a reliable person.

Visibility: Make your contributions known

Make sure people in leadership roles can see your professional contributions. Your uniqueness might not be noticed if your contributions are hidden, your role is not visible, or if you don't take credit when it is due to you. If you rarely receive direct feedback on your contributions, that is a good indication that your contribution might not be visible. Ask yourself: Who in your organization knows what you do? If the answer is limited to those who are not in key roles, you need to make yourself more visible. Only you can determine the best way to gain more visibility appropriately, without appearing pushy, threatening, or arrogant. Here are a few suggestions:

Ask. Getting more visibility is often as simple as just asking your supervisor for it. You could try asking something like: "Do you think I might be able to sit in on the meeting when you present the designs to the client? I am curious to see their reaction, and it will help me learn how to give client presentations myself in the future." Or possibly: "Would I be able to attend one of your weekly update meetings this quarter? I'd like to learn more about how you connect the dots with the other units. It would help me better understand our business."

Accept the credit you deserve. This suggestion is more challenging if you have been socialized in a culture where modesty and humility is prized. Do you find it difficult to use the phrase "I did" and prefer to say "we did" even when you acted alone? If so, this piece of advice is for you. Start small: When someone compliments you, simply say "thank you" and nothing else. If a colleague says, "that was a great report," say "thank you." If you are modest to a fault, this will not be easy. Practice. Once you get over your discomfort with accepting compliments, you can start to work your way up to talking about your accomplishments and comfortably receiving credit for what you do well. As an aside, some people need no advice on professional boasting, and, at times, take it too far. They sign into video conferences with a name like "Pat who did such a great job on the last quarterly presentation." We don't recommend that. We are not trying to create more organizational egomaniacs. Rather, we want you to be proud of the excellent work you do, credit and all.

Post. LinkedIn is a great place to post your accomplishments to your professional network. If you are using the site correctly, your coworkers and leaders in your organization will be part of your network.

Excellence: Be known for high-quality work

Execute your tasks with excellence. The best evidence of your performance should be others' response to your work product, which will come in a variety of forms such as compliments or complaints, messages, informal feedback, and formal performance reviews. If you aren't sure, don't wait for an annual performance review to meter whether your work product is excellent. Make a habit of asking your supervisor and other trusted colleagues for suggestions, honest feedback on ways to improve. One of the best ways to ask is with simple questions such as "how could I have been even more effective in . . .?" It takes some humility but is well worth the effort.

Performing with excellence might mean putting in extra effort if you are not there yet. You might need to practice a presentation at home in front of a mirror. You might need to do some additional research, take an online course, or bring work home on your own time. The possibilities to help you execute your visible roles flawlessly are as varied as the jobs that exist. The bottom line is to be great at what you do—whatever it is.

Organizational culture and your ideal career

Organizations have cultures, and your ability to fit in and thrive within that culture can affect your ability to succeed in it. It is important to take your time to really understand your future employer's organizational culture because it will influence your career. Research has found that employees will have higher job satisfaction, better performance, and lower strain in organizations with an empowerment culture.[4]

One way to assess an organizational culture is to observe those who are successful in the organization. Among the most successful, do you sense similarities in how they behave, their values, communication styles, and the like? If the answer is "yes," try to note what is similar among them. Do you value what they seem to value? Are their behaviors comfortable representations of your own? If you do not share the values you see at the top of the organization, conforming might lead to a promotion, but might not to your fulfillment.

Before you join an organization, we want you to assess—really look deeply—at the behaviors and attitudes of your future supervisor, teammates, leaders, and anyone else who has been with this employer for over one year. They will likely be the standard-bearers of the organizational culture. While there should be room for you to be yourself in the best organization, it is also true that, over time, you will become more like those in the company than they will become like you. Take your time with this step as it is often the case that the nuances of a corporate culture are unspoken and socialized but not found in any written company policy.

At Tamr, for example, Andy has used a framework that he believes in deeply: where values are at the core and guide behaviors. The collective behaviors of everyone at Tamr define the culture.

Tamr's core values are:

- Diversity & Inclusion: Broader perspectives yield better outcomes
- Communication: Be open and honest (even when it's hard)
- Grounded Trust: Trust but verify
- Humility: There is always room for improvement
- Attitude: Nothing is impossible
- Teamwork: Team sport on every dimension

The behaviors that Tamr aspires to reinforce include:

- Put Customers First: Strive to delight
- Move Fast: Perfect is the enemy of good enough
- Play as a Team: Disagree and commit (no talking behind people's backs)
- Bottom-Up, Data-Driven: In God we trust; everyone else bring data
- Behave Ethically: Treat others as you would like to be treated

Tamr describes its culture as:

- Welcoming: New hires, interns, customers
- Collaborative: Within and across teams, internal and external
- High Expectations: Of ourselves, each other, and our customers/ partners
- Risk-Embracing: Support bold endeavors

As new people join Tamr, they are guided by the Tamr core values but also exhibit their own personal behaviors, some consistent, some not. Andy notes that at Tamr "we adjust to new people and behaviors. We're constantly tuning and evolving our culture to meet the changing needs of our business. Values don't change all that often, but behaviors to align with those values are constantly evolving."

Professional style and your ideal career

Even at the most senior levels of organizations, we have watched numerous technically excellent managers derail before reaching the executive suite because they were deemed to not have "executive presence." It is a frustrating piece of feedback to tell bright, competent managers that they "lack executive presence" without giving any clarity on what is meant by this. The Center for Talent Innovation[5] found that executive presence has three unequally weighted components: gravitas (confidence, decisiveness, vision, authenticity, integrity), communication (written and verbal), and appearance. Unlike what many people think, appearance is only one small piece of executive presence. The bulk of what makes people appear to have executive presence is their gravitas or their demeanor, attitudes, and behaviors. That spot on your lapel might not be a disqualifying mark in your executive interview, but an inability to enunciate your vision for the future might be (but it's still good to try and get the spot out before the interview).

Appearance alone isn't it, so you won't be able to don your company's version of a power outfit and be automatically knighted with executive presence. It is not yours to claim. It is evaluated by others who meet you, their opinions being formed both quickly and over time. Research[6] has found that some elements of executive presence are formed within *the first five minutes of meeting*, such as status, projected confidence, communication skills, and engagement, while others, including integrity, power use, intellect, and expertise, are evaluated over time.

Many people have the gravitas (high in integrity, vision, intellect, etc.) to be perceived as having executive presence. To get to the point when people will see your wonderful attributes, you still need to get through the first five minutes to be certain you are being perceived in the way you would hope. Here are three things that can help move the needle on your executive presence.

Have a pulled-together look (whatever your look might be). As a tech CEO, Andy's power outfit is jeans and a white long-sleeved shirt or a sweatshirt. It is the look that sends the right image and works well at his company. Paula likes to dress as her MBA students might expect to see a senior business professional wearing, even though academics are not the most fashion-forward group. She loves a professional, but feminine, look. Our looks are very different, but they are both intentional: personal choice mixed with organizational norms while maintaining a pulled-together look.

Improve your communication skills. We have seen many brilliant people who are unable to reach their next desired level in their career because they are unable to effectively communicate their thoughts (usually orally). The solution generally involves coaching on communication, public speaking, and presentation skills. Practicing in front of a mirror or with your dog can help build your confidence.

Project confidence. Some technically gifted people are stifled in their career acts because of their own timidity. Whether real or perceived, they give the sense to others that they are unsure about their work, opinions, and decisions. These individuals can work on their ability to exude vibes of confidence, to present themselves as a person in control. This can be achieved through improving verbal skills and learning to present oneself assertively with other small behavioral changes, such as posture and eye contact.

After you have buffed and polished yourself, you now need to find your center for attraction. Identifying a center for attraction and developing it is far more difficult to coach because it is generally a function of the person's natural charm, graceful calm, energetic charisma, quiet ease, or some other quality that might be difficult to pinpoint. It is your "X factor." Some individuals remain brilliant in their technical or functional areas but are not deemed to be promotable highfliers within their chosen organization because they do not possess one of these leadership qualities. The goal is to find your most natural style and amplify it in a way that gives you a leader-like quality.

If leadership is part of your ideal career and you believe that executive presence might matter, behave in ways that others can easily visualize you in the role. The changes, if you are honest with yourself about the behaviors that need to be altered, might be relatively straightforward. *The big question is whether you want to change for the sake of your career.* If the answer is "no," you should find a career act where you will be appreciated and rewarded for being exactly who you want to be, wearing what you want to wear, communicating as you want to communicate, and so on. *You see the pattern, right?* Your career journey toward your ideal career is all about you and what you, not your employer, find fulfilling about the way you work. That said, don't shy away from solid coaching that will help you throughout your career journey. Being authentic is not the same as running in place. It is identifying your core traits and amplifying them.

Company politics and your ideal career

Within organizations of all sizes, there are political realities and shifts in power. No matter how critical, unique, reliable, visible, and excellent you are, you might fall victim to organizational changes beyond your control, such as mergers, acquisitions, reorganizations, and divestitures. Even a change of personnel in a level above you might result in a personality clash or simply the loss of a supportive supervisor. These are to be expected when working for an organization. Keep your ear to the ground, so to speak, to learn what is happening before it is formally announced in your organization.

Office or organizational politics produce more challenging shifts to the environment because they are less obvious to those who are not pulling the political strings. Political alliances often form when people try to gain power through their networks, creating in-groups and out-groups among employees. Many people who engage in office politics are trying to get some of their fundamental needs met such as the need to grow their competence, have autonomy, or create their in-group to satiate their need for relatedness.[7] Regardless of whether you know this is happening, you might find yourself aligned with the wrong group when the political wind shifts. This is unfortunate for those who are swept along unsuspectingly because they did not realize they were being co-opted into a political alliance in the first place.

Most people don't like office politics. Meta-analysis has shown that employees don't like it when their work environment is saturated in office politics and that managers and organizations need to work to mitigate damage associated from office politics.[8] Even in these more enlightened organizations, it will help you to understand the politics of your organization.

To navigate through the shifting winds of office politics, try to work effectively across multiple organizational groups (including divisions, levels, or functional areas). Be a person who understands the political dynamics but does not play them if it can be avoided. Don't be "that person" who tries too hard to play politics, rather than utilizing their personal competence, to get ahead. At the other extreme, do not be oblivious to the fact that politics exist. But be aware: Both ends of this continuum usually run into trouble at some point in their careers. The following are a few pieces of advice about organizational politics:

- **Do not be blind to office politics.** They exist everywhere; some places are more political than others but there will always be alliances among people and shifts in power and influence. If you ignore politics completely, you will be viewed as naïve.

- **Avoid being toxically political yourself.** Once you understand office politics, you might need to flow with them. You cannot stop breathing the air in the room and expect to survive. Nonetheless, do not make the organizational culture more closed or uncomfortable by trying to hoard resources and relationships. If you are doing that, you are part of the problem. In the most toxically political places, knowledge is hoarded and shared sparingly with only the right people. Don't do that.

- **Try to anticipate the political changes.** Just as the tightrope walker is about to step on the banana peel, you don't want to miss a change coming in your environment. Listen. Talk to your mentor. Ask questions. Try to get some confirmation from multiple reliable sources.

- **Know how you are perceived with respect to political alliances.** We've both seen very senior managers and outstanding performers fall out of favor politically and lose power. This scenario is less upsetting when politics were played and the winds shifted—and far more upsetting when apolitical people are perceived to be aligned, without intention or knowledge, because they shared an interest (e.g., carpooled or ran together at lunch) and had become friends outside of work.

Exercise: Assess the strength of your safety net

We know that a single career act can be risky without the suggestions in the previous section. You can assess the strength of your own safety net by diagnosing your organization's stability, the criticality and uniqueness of your role, and your job performance in your role. Test your safety net by using the following exercise.

RISK FACTOR #1: ASSESS YOUR <u>ORGANIZATION'S STABILITY</u>

Check any of the following you have observed in your organization:

- ☐ There is a hiring freeze announced.
- ☐ There is a freeze on nonessential travel.
- ☐ Open positions are quietly not being filled while duties are transferred to others.
- ☐ Temporary contracts are not being renewed.
- ☐ Your company was recently acquired.

If you have more than two of these checked, *your organization's stability* is a risk factor.

RISK FACTOR #2: ASSESS YOUR <u>ROLE</u>

Check any of the following that seem to describe your role:

- ☐ I am in a support role, as opposed to a line role.
- ☐ My role does not directly create wealth for the organization (i.e., I am neither making nor selling for the employer).
- ☐ The company could still be competitive, even without someone in my role.
- ☐ My skills are relatively easy to find in the labor market.
- ☐ I could be easily replaced.

If you have more than two of these checked, *your role* is a risk factor.

RISK FACTOR #3: ASSESS YOUR JOB PERFORMANCE

Check any of the following that describe your job performance:

- ☐ My most recent performance rating has been less than perfect.
- ☐ I am occasionally late for work.
- ☐ My work is occasionally criticized.
- ☐ There are better-performing employees holding my same job title.
- ☐ Some people would say I am a difficult person to work with.

If you have more than two of these checked, *your job performance* is a risk factor.

HOW MANY OF THE THREE RISK FACTORS DO YOU HAVE?

If you have no risk factors, the likelihood that you will lose your job is probably low. Revisit this periodically to assess whether the situation has changed.

If you have one risk factor, there is some risk that you might lose your job. If you like your organization and your only risk factor is your role, you might want to consider whether there is a more central or core position in your organization where your skills can be applied. The more you are in a critical role, the safer your job. Likewise, you might want to gain additional high-demand skills as the additional skills will make you more difficult to replace. The risk factor over which you have the greatest control is your job performance. If this is a concern, you might want to recommit yourself to performing reliably and with excellence in your role.

If you have two or three risk factors, you have some reason to be concerned. You might want to proactively begin to look for another job while you still have one.

We end this chapter the same way we started it: by reminding you that the riskiest of all career acts is the single career act within an organization. To lower the risk, be certain to maintain CURVE in your role (i.e., critical, unique, reliable, visible, and excellent) to give you the best possible safety net. While with your employer, be certain to focus on your career journey and the type of experiences needed to move closer to your ideal career.

KEY TAKEAWAYS

- If you are working for an organization, occupy career acts where you are in critical and unique roles.
- Perform your roles with reliability, visibility, and excellence.
- Understand the organizational environment. Organizational culture, professional style, and company politics can have an influence on your career journey within the company.
- Be able to assess your position's risk factors and continue your career journey when the current situation is too risky for you to continue your career development.

SOCIAL MEDIA CHALLENGES

These challenges are a way to showcase how you *Live for a Living* by offering advice on what is working for you on your career journey. While creating your personal brand, your posts can also inspire those in your network to achieve their career goals. By assisting others in this way, you might even enjoy an endorphin boost (the "helper's high") from the knowledge that you are helping others succeed. Post these to Instagram, Facebook, LinkedIn, or whatever social media platform you use. When you post, please tag #LiveforaLiving and the hashtag for the challenge.

1. #WorkingSmarter

Share a short video or photo montage to highlight the ways you are working smarter. You can showcase your workspace, what you do when you work, or any other elements from your professional life that demonstrate the positive changes you have made. You can inspire others to emulate the changes you have made.

2. #DayInTheLifeOf

Share your day through a video or series of photos. Show your network a behind-the-scenes view into your workday, especially what makes your career positive for you. You could include any daily routine, your workspace, your interactions with colleagues, and any part of your day that represents what you do and why you like it.

3. #BestCareerAdvice

Offer the most valuable piece of career advice you have been given and how it helped you achieve your goal. Create a short video or a post to share a tip or strategy that worked for you and how it might help others in their own career journey.

continued

4. #FulfillingCareer

Share a message explaining why you feel fulfilled in your career. You might want to describe what you do, what makes you proud, and how it puts you into a state of flow. You should share the challenges and more difficult parts of the career too. Your post might inspire others to join the same career, so be sure to be realistic about it.

PART 3

CREATE
MOMENTUM

CHAPTER 7

INTEGRATE YOUR
LIFE PRIORITIES
WITH YOUR CAREER

Action expresses priorities.

—GANDHI

If you've been at a high-profile event or fundraiser in the Boston, Massa-chusetts, area recently and heard people raving over the confections being served, you're likely eating (or perhaps still looking at) the work of Andrea Theodorakos, also known as the Cookie Goddess.[1]

Half artist, half pastry chef, and all-in wife, mother, and solopreneur, Andrea started Cookie Goddess Cakes in 2010 as a creative outlet and source of extra income.

Growing up in a traditional, first-generation Greek-American house-hold, Andrea understood that her main job would be that of a wife and mother. And, although she attended college, she in fact chose to be a full-time, hands-on mother to her son and daughter as they navigated their childhood years. Her artistic flair, legendary entertaining skills, vivacious personality, and love of baking enjoyed an enthusiastic but limited audi-ence in the home and her local community.

With her children growing up—"they decided they didn't want a heli-copter mother" she laughs—she sought another outlet for her creative energy.

Two pivotal life events also nudged her. First, her father died, leaving her mother, a homemaker and highly intelligent woman with financial security, struggling to function alone. Second, as her daughter moved toward wom-anhood and independence, Andrea realized that she deserved a better role model. "How could I encourage my daughter to pursue her dreams and take advantage of the opportunities open to her if I weren't doing this myself?" she says. "I wanted to show her that I can do what I absolutely adore, but I can also be there for her if she needs me for any reason, as well as my husband or my son or my mom."

Building on her skills and her baking hobby, Andrea started a home-based business selling her locally famous cookies. (An earlier idea, making and selling gift baskets, had proved untenable at the time.) The business took off day one, powered completely by word-of-mouth (no paid advertising).

The Internet became her silent business partner, keeping founding and operating costs low. Social media, then in its early days, gave Andrea an efficient way to reach a broader regional market, without having to create a full-fledged e-commerce website. She started posting pictures of her cook-ies online and then taking incoming orders over her company Facebook page by email and phone. She added Internet payment options (Venmo and Square) and Internet banking as soon as they became available. More recently, Instagram, which is linked to her Facebook page, became a showroom for her gorgeous edible works. She's experimented with new products and packaging. Complete strangers on Facebook have become her mentors and sources of ideas.

Today, Andrea's highly personalized, imaginatively designed cookies are often a dominant part of the themes at events and celebrations. For a corpo-rate event involving Sports Illustrated swimsuit cover model Camille Kotsek, Andrea designed cookies replicating her cover—to the delight of Ms. Kotsek and her partner, legendary New England Patriots tight end Rob Gronkowski, and other guests. "Seeing 'Gronk' waving his cookie and saying 'This is just like Christmas!' was definitely a career highlight," she says. As was the wedding of a local broadcaster and her fireman husband—with cookies bearing a microphone and firetruck, respectively. But every client's celebration, no matter how big or small, and every product gets Andrea's personal attention and her heart: her brand promise.

A self-confessed "Type A," Andrea is known for her meticulous attention to detail. Before she bakes anything, she makes detailed sketches of her concepts until she gets it just right. She does everything herself, right down to packaging every product before she delivers it, or the customer picks it up. And she has no plans to add staff.

For now, Andrea has a perfect business for her: doing something that she absolutely loves, it provides a creative outlet and can accommodate her other job (wife and mother). It gives her an income stream that she independently controls, enabling her to contribute to the household budget, occasionally help a relative in Greece replace a broken refrigerator, and/or invest in other things important to her.

Although it's a one-person, home-based operation, she runs it with Fortune 500 efficiency.

While cookies are still on the menu, Andrea in recent years has shifted the product line toward cakes. While her cakes, in many respects, are less taxing to make and more lucrative, they take special artistry and some engineering skill. Andrea's cakes are distinctive, memorable, and definitely for life's most special events. "These are not your typical sheet cakes," she says. "My cakes aren't for your twenty-second birthday. They're for your twenty-first." She continues to push the edge of the envelope in her work, including her very popular 3D cakes.

Like all businesses, Andrea's had to pivot during COVID-19. With bar and bat mitzvahs (a staple of her business) and nearly all other special events canceled, orders for her cakes were initially way down. So, she bumped up the cookie business. She created complete individual cookie coloring kits that could help entertain kids while they were home from school (very popular and a repeat, subscription-like business.) She instituted no-touch pickup and delivery. She helped clients create touch-free, drive-by kid's birthday parties, with individually packaged birthday cupcakes that went home with celebrants.

With her busiest time being everyone else's party time (the November-to-January holiday season), she's become a military-grade planner. She delivers and accompanies her cakes to most events. By January, she's wearing an arm brace against a creeping case of arthritis.

Being a solopreneur has had its challenges. In the early days, pricing her products for what they were truly worth was challenging ("It took me some time to convince myself that my time was worth money," she says). As was the decision to take on wedding cakes. "I was terrified with my first wedding cake, because I knew that it was the centerpiece of the wedding, that the couple was going to be photographed in front of this wedding cake and that their grandchildren would look at it," she says. Not to mention the transportation requirements and other business practicalities.

With an estimated thousand cakes behind her, Andrea has no plans to hang up her apron. "I feel like I'm contributing to my family. My work also brings a nice element to my friendships and to my family, and I'm proud of that," she says. "I think I'm prouder of the fact that I did it on my own, and I didn't do it on anyone's coattails. It was 100% me. That's why I take so much pride in every cookie and every cake, because it is a representation of me."

Even without a sweet tooth, you can admire the fulfillment Andrea exudes from her career. If she won millions in the lottery tomorrow, do you think she would never bake again? If Andrea is like most people who find deep fulfillment from their work, probably not.

How about you? If you won $4 million in a lottery today, would you still want to have a career? Drs. Richard Arvey, Itzhak Harpaz, and Hui Liao found that lottery winners (average winning almost $4 million) do not automatically quit working.[2] They found that about 85 percent of them continue working in some form. The level of centrality and importance work plays in the lottery winners' lives factored into their decision regarding whether to continue working. These researchers note that "although individuals may have continued to work, they also may have modified the type and conditions of their work experiences (e.g., by starting another business or by dropping to part-time work)." In other words, they worked in ways that were consistent with their work-related values and the goals they had for their careers.

If you are reading this, it means that you have read a book on finding more fulfillment from your career. Like the high-dollar lottery winners who continued working, you might also be the type of person who wants to focus on the stimulation that can be gained from a fulfilling career. Also, like the high-dollar lottery winners, you want a stimulating career, but you want it on your terms, consistent with your career-related values and leaving enough time and emotional resources for those you love.

While easier, you do not need to win the lottery to make this happen. You do, however, need to satisfy your work-related values *in the context of your other life priorities, especially your loved ones.* Both parts are important and covered in this chapter:

1. Your career-related values

2. The priorities you have across all spheres of your life, especially your loved ones

Having an amazing career at the cost of loving relationships, your well-being, or your nonwork interests will not create the fulfilling life you seek. There is no easy recipe or pithy "if-then" advice to be found in this chapter. We do, however, provide plenty of room for personal insights and self-awareness.

This chapter needs time to digest. Sit under a tree or lock yourself in the bathroom—anywhere you can to think. Clear your head of distractions, be present, and read on.

Your values and your career

Your journey toward that ideal career will be smoother and more fulfilling when it aligns with your core work-related values. Your work values will propel you to select certain careers and will help you remain in and be satisfied with careers which align with your values. They set your priorities and serve as a GPS in your journey. Values give you that gut instinct and "little voice inside your head" reminding you of your core beliefs and attitudes. Ignoring your work-related values is like ignoring your GPS when it is trying to give you directions. You might get there eventually but you took a rougher route and probably burned more gas (or whatever you're using to fuel your journey).

VISIT MYJOURNII.COM

Complete the Assessment to Build Awareness of Your Work Values

You can use this diagnostic to better understand your work values and how they should be integrated into your career choices.

We spoke about values as they pertained to *how* you prefer to work in previous chapters. As you might recall, these work values can be *intrinsic*, the values that move us to self-motivate (e.g., using one's creativity or opportunities for learning), or extrinsic (e.g., compensation, job security). They can also be *status-oriented* (e.g., span of authority or level in the hierarchy) or *socially oriented* (e.g., working for the greater good or with people).

As your career journey unfolds, your work values will manifest in many ways, such as how many hours per day you will work, how much you are willing to work from home, whether you make friends with colleagues from work, whether you prioritize work over leisure time, and the like. While these values can be influenced by family, education, and national culture, research has found that the rank-order of these values remain relatively stable throughout one's career.[3] If they are with us throughout our careers, it is probably better to not ignore them.

Now, let's consider the values affecting *the way your career intersects in other aspects of your life.* There are three values to consider:

- **Work centrality:** How important is your work to your overall life satisfaction and personal identity? To what extent is *what you do* important to you, maybe even defining *who you are*? If you are a lottery winner with high work centrality, you may still want to work because to stop working would threaten or change your identity in an uncomfortable or undesirable way. On the other hand, if you are lower in work centrality, disassociating from work could be easier for you. It will be easier for you to change in and out of work and nonwork roles more comfortably. What happens at work doesn't influence you as much. Research found that people who are higher in work centrality find that unfulfilling or boring work affects their mood, making them more depressed.[4] They especially need a more rewarding career journey.

- **Achievement orientation:** Your achievement orientation, ambition, or personal drive to succeed is also an important career-related value. This manifests in how hard you are willing to push to succeed, how many risks you are willing to take to achieve your career goals, and how high the goals are that you set for yourself. If you are a strongly achievement-oriented lottery winner, you will likely continue working toward "stretch" career goals even though you don't need the money. If your achievement orientation is less salient, you might choose to change careers and do something requiring less of your time and energy.

- **Comfort with work/life overlap:** The comfort level you have allowing the spheres of your life to comingle influences your preferences for harmonizing your career with your family life and social life. Are you someone who places a high value on keeping your personal affairs to yourself when you are at work? To the extent that you socialize with your business colleagues, do you see them separately from your personal friends and family? Or, at the other end of the scale, do you make a point of sharing significant events and people in your personal life with your business colleagues? A lottery winner, someone with low work/life overlap would probably keep his or her newfound financial freedom confidential. Someone who has an affinity for high work/life overlap might enjoy nothing better than to start a new business, owned and operated by family and close friends.

There is no "correct" answer here. We could not recommend any level of work centrality, achievement orientation, and comfort with work/life overlap any more than we would recommend which sports team or music genre you should like. Each value is unique to you. These values shape the decisions you make on how your career seeps into the other spheres of your life. The more aware you are of how you hold these values, the better you can make career decisions that you will move you closer to an ideal career that fits with your life's priorities.

The more you understand your own career-related values, the more consciously you will be able to use them to navigate career-related decisions. If you are in an early phase of your career journey, you might need some time and experience before you are able to say what your career-related values are. If you are in a later phase, you might see your values beginning to change. Values can form and change over time as the circumstances of our lives change.

Your career and your loved ones

It is important to understand your career values and how they influence your relationships with those you love as you engage in your career journey. *Have you heard anyone praising a loved one using any of the following sentiments?*

"I am so proud of ___. ___ just received a big promotion at work."

"___'s business is doing well. ___ has worked so hard to build that business to what it is today."

"I am so glad ___ left his/her company. The money is not worth the sacrifice."

"I give ___ so much credit for going back to school. It will be difficult for us, but it is important to ___."

These are all positive sentiments expressed by those who admire and respect the career-related values of their loved ones. Each statement also reflects the way in which the person they are praising should manage their career. When statements like these are uttered by those we love and they align with our own self-concept, there is a positive and reinforcing synergy. If you hear comments that don't align with your self-concept, like "Why would you ever want to work *there*?" just smile, take a deep breath, and change the subject.

Your life partner/spouse, more than anyone else, will have the greatest influence later in your life. At minimum, how you spend your time will be shaped, directly or indirectly, by your partner. *Who does the cooking? Who helps kids with homework? Who takes on extra household duties while the other is working on a big work project?* Time becomes a shared resource. This isn't a small issue—especially for those who start their lives together at an early stage of their careers, when there are fewer demands on one's time.

Let us provide an illustration of how this plays out with one couple, Helen and Tim. Helen and Tim are fictitious characters who have been fused from the very real stories of dozens of couples we have met over the years. We could change their roles, names, and genders, but the story's trajectory would remain the same.

Helen and Tim met and fell in love when they were college students. They were introduced through mutual friends, and quickly found that they had many interests and values in common. They were a loving and respectful couple, communicating well with each other. After graduation, Tim (with his management degree) started working as an assistant manager for a branch of a car rental company. Helen (with her engineering degree) began an entry-level job working in research and development for a medical devices company. Two years after graduation, they were married. As newlyweds, Tim and Helen were not only in love but also very happy with the starter phase of their respective careers and their new life together.

Prior to their engagement, Tim and Helen had serious conversations about their financial values (both are fiscally conservative), family values (both wanted children), and faith. But unfortunately, they were so new to their careers that their career-related values were still forming. They never discussed their work-related values because they did not know what they were—or even that there was such a thing.

By the time they had been married for a year, it became clear that Tim had a lower career centrality and achievement orientation than Helen; he also had a low tolerance for work/life overlap. He worked hard and was promoted, but Helen felt he lacked a zest for work and did not devote enough energy to planning his future career moves. In Helen's eyes, Tim liked having a job that paid well but it was "just a job." In contrast, as Helen became more involved in her career, she became more and more identified with her job. She had no problem bringing work home with her. In fact, Helen loved the discovery process of her job—the greater the challenge, the more she enjoyed the work. She frequently described how she could not "turn off her brain when she went home" when she was trying to work through an engineering challenge. And this was an annoyance to Tim, who wanted Helen to join him in relaxing and enjoying their leisure time when they were not at work.

Tim and Helen could not understand each other's positions and began to resent each other. Helen thought Tim was "settling" and did not care about his career. Tim thought Helen did not have her priorities right and was giving too much of herself to her job. Both complained that the other partner had "changed" and was not the same person they married. After just three years of marriage, they filed for a divorce, citing irreconcilable differences.

Young couples who marry in their early twenties (ages twenty through twenty-four) have a divorce risk of almost 40 percent.[5] The American Academy of Matrimonial Lawyers lists "dramatic change in priorities" as one of the top reasons couples of all ages cite for divorcing.[6] Helen and Tim, unfortunately, illustrate both statistics.

Whether as a symptom or a reason for the breakup, the ability to communicate about work-related values would save much heartache. It is important that you are communicating regarding your career-related values. This does not mean that you must share every value. It does not even mean that you must know what your values are. What it does mean is that you find a way to work out the boundaries in a way that will be comfortable for both of you.

Setting these boundaries begins with a conversation, an open discussion about how you and your partner will navigate potential differences and maximize each other's professional goals, rooted in love and respect for the other's journey. While these conversations are not always easy, they are worth the effort. Paula and her colleagues conducted a study on families that had been relocated internationally for one partner's job.[7] As you can imagine, it was an incredible disruption for the entire family to be pulled, roots and all, from their home country to a host country for a few years. We found that family support, family communication, and family adaptability predicted the performance of the person working in the host country. The work done ahead of time to make this a worthwhile experience for the family ultimately had a positive career outcome.

Your values will likely change over time and so will those of your partner. On some values, you might be evenly matched, whereas on others, you might be at opposite extremes. Research has a powerful example of value alignment. In a study of couples[8] in which both partners were higher in work centrality, it was found that they cared for and supported each other and participated in fun activities together, giving them both the ability to recharge. Together, these couples worked hard, played together, and supported each other.

Matching is not necessarily better than being opposites; many couples find that their different work-related values complement each other and make their relationship even richer and more satisfying. Whatever your work-related values are and however they evolve, remember that for a great career, you need to communicate with those you love, for your nearest and dearest are not on the sidelines of your career—they are an integral part of your life, which includes your career.

Mindfulness across all the spheres of your life

There isn't a magic number—the perfect percentage of time—to harmonize your career with the other priorities in your life. While we can't offer a number, we can offer a technique that has worked for both of us: be fully present or "in the moment" wherever you are, whether at work, at home, playing sports, with your partner, or caring for your children. This quality of being fully present is something Buddhists call "mindfulness"; it is the opposite of "going through the motions" or "acting on autopilot."

Even if you are the most career-oriented person, work is only one sphere of your life. For many people, their family life, their social life, and their private or personal life (including the activities such as hobbies, sports, recreational activities, and participation in a faith community) are the three most important spheres along with their careers. Understanding your career values and practicing mindfulness in all the activities of your life helps to bring those you love with you as you enjoy your career.

Have any of these ever happened to you:

- You are reading the news or a book but not absorbing the content because you are thinking about what is happening in the next room.

- You are watching your child's softball game, but your mind is on what you need to do tomorrow at work.

- You are at the dinner table with your spouse but planning your morning staff meeting.

- You are on the phone with a loved one, but rather than listening, you are thinking about the shopping you need to do after the call.

This happens to all of us—some more than others. It is not because we love our work more than our children's softball games. It is not because we care more about shopping than our loved one's conversation. It is because many career-oriented people are future goal-oriented and have difficulty living in the moment and being mindful. The goal has a greater pull than the present moment. It is possible to go from this mental multitasking to a more focused mental mono-tasking. If you are a practicing Buddhist or meditate regularly, you know this already. Skip ahead. If you are like the rest of us, you really need to read this section carefully.

Psychologists Kirk Warren Brown and Richard Ryan[9] found that mindfulness increases individuals' psychological well-being and lowers stress. They, along with other researchers, characterize mindfulness as being a higher quality of consciousness. And consciousness has two components: awareness and attention. As such, being mindful, or fully present, will have the added benefits of allowing you to offer more of yourself to those you love and improving your own well-being.

The two concepts around being mindful *seem* straightforward enough:

1. *Be aware* of the present.

2. *Be attentive* and focus your awareness to that which matters most.

Think of the practice of mindfulness as a flashlight beam. Direct your attention light beam to the situation and then focus the beam so the intensity of the awareness shines only on whatever deserves your attention (your child stealing second base; the news story you are reading). These two concepts seem easy in theory but tend to be difficult in practice for most people. Being mindful and present in the nonwork spheres of your life are especially challenging for those who are getting their bursts of dopamine from their work. If mindfulness is not a natural strength, your stimulating career might be getting more of your mental resources than you think it is. For you, being fully attentive in the nonwork spheres of life will take practice.

There are many books written about ways to improve mindfulness. Applying the advice to your career, we encourage you to try (or at least start with) the following:

- **Consciously decide to increase your mindfulness.** Make mindfulness a conscious decision in the nonwork spheres of your life. For example, before dinner, think about the activity of being fully present at the dinner table. During the meal, if your attention starts to drift, try to catch yourself and bring your attention and awareness back to where you are. If someone asks if the main course needs more salt, "I like the way it's seasoned" is a much more mindful answer than, "I still don't understand why they promoted Roger." Particularly if you're having dinner with Roger. Be intentional about making an extra effort to do this whenever you are engaging, even in the most mundane situations.

- **Clear the mental decks.** If there is something pressing that will keep you from focusing your attention, try to clear your mental deck before engaging with your loved ones. For example, do not return your loved one's call in the middle of the day when you know you will have many things on your mind. Instead, wait for a time when there is a lull, so it is easier to be fully present. Similarly, a sweet way to start a date night is by making a point of turning off your phone. To some, that is more romantic than flowers. Paula thinks both are appropriate.

- **Engage the active moments.** If you stay present in the moments requiring your interaction, you will learn more about the details of the lives of your loved ones and derive more intense emotions from the experience. Get into the habit of asking sincere and nonjudgmental questions about what your loved one is doing or discussing. For example, as you stay "in the moment" during a conversation, try not to evaluate but instead to listen and inquire out of curiosity and a desire for clarification. Asking such questions will encourage your active attention and help you to empathize more fully with your loved one.

- **Savor the passive moment.** Mindfulness encourages us to be present and savor the simplest moments of our lives: the feeling of the water in the shower, the taste of our toast in the morning, the fragrance of the garden when we arrive home. Starting from a more basic place, savor the moments you have with your spouse or partner, children, extended family, and friends. Enjoy the experience of playing a sport or engaging in a hobby. As you practice the habit of focusing more of your attention and awareness on the experience, you will become more present.

- **Take nothing for granted.** Simple acts of kindness, compassion, and gratitude also help focus us more on the moments in all the spheres of our lives. If you remember to say "thank you" and be grateful for the simplest of things, you can more fully experience the simplest of things.

Added benefits are always worth highlighting. Increasing mindfulness has been shown to have a benefit to your career as well as your personal life.

A review of the vast academic literature[10] on the benefits of mindfulness has found that people who are more mindful are also better performers and better organizational citizens. Mindful people tend to be more highly rated in conflict management, leadership, and teamwork. With something so beneficial for all the spheres of your life, it is a skill worth developing. Oh, and it's free.

Unbridled enthusiasm for your career can be energy-giving and fulfilling. It is, remember, only one sphere of your life. We want you to enjoy the journey and have a fulfilling and love-filled life. Your career does not need to operate in opposition to the other spheres of your life. You never want to leave your loved ones in the wake of a career; you want them to enjoy the ride—and a great life—with you.

KEY TAKEAWAYS

- Your career-related values (work centrality, achievement orientation, comfort with work/life overlap) will affect the way your career will intersect in other aspects of your life. Understanding these will influence the other priorities in your life (e.g., family, friends, hobbies).

- It is important to understand your career-related values and how they influence your relationships with those you love as you engage in your career journey.

- Have open communication with your loved ones, especially your life partner, on your career-related values and how to weave them comfortably into your collective life.

- Many career-oriented people are future goal-oriented and have difficulty living in the moment, detracting from their work/life harmony.

- Mindfulness benefits both the work and the nonwork spheres of your life.

CHAPTER 8

LEVERAGE YOUR TIME AND MONEY

We never know the worth of water till the well is dry.
—ENGLISH PROVERB

Serial entrepreneurs and dynamic husband-and-wife team Elizabeth Lawler and Kevin Gilpin in 2013 co-founded Conjur, a cybersecurity company that was acquired by CyberArk in 2017.[1] Letting no time pass, in 2019 they co-founded AppMap, a company that visualizes, analyzes, and continuously improves software quality at the speed of modern development. Today, Elizabeth and Kevin are in the give-back phase of their careers, serving as board members and angel investors while running AppMap.

Well-educated and highly accomplished, Elizabeth holds a PhD in epidemiology from Boston University and has a background in data science and software development. She worked for the Department of Veterans Affairs, where she developed software for the healthcare system. Kevin is a "10X" (wildly productive) software engineer with a background in aerospace engineering. He worked in various tech companies, including Trilogy, I2, Infinity Pharmaceuticals, and more.

Together, Elizabeth and Kevin's unique backgrounds in data science and software development in regulated environments equipped them with the skills and knowledge necessary to build great products from scratch (R&D). But there was more to their career story than just exceptional talent. Elizabeth and Kevin met while attending their respective colleges in the Boston area, connecting years later professionally (by chance) and soon thereafter marrying. With their combined energy and mutual belief in an emerging challenge (enabling software to securely write other software), they presciently started Conjur on a card table in their living room. Specifically, they foresaw a growing gap in the market for a security system that could handle the complexities of cloud-based infrastructure. Conjur was thus born.

Elizabeth and Kevin put their expertise, unique skills, time, and money into "bootstrapping" Conjur. When they first started the company, money and resources were tight. Each juggled multiple consulting jobs, plowing everything back into the company. Later, they literally "bet the farm" on their product idea, taking a second mortgage on the small Massachusetts farmhouse in which they lived. The partners took a thoughtful, conservative approach to how they managed the company's time and money resources—something that did not go unnoticed by outside investors, partners, and customers. (At one point, Elizabeth's business card read "Resourceress"—emphasizing her role in creatively finding and managing the skills, operations, and funds needed to bring a technical product to market on the right timeline and budget.)

Today, they continue to run a lean shop in whatever they do, even though they now have more personal resources that they can invest. In 2017 Conjur was acquired by CyberArk, a global leader in privileged access security. The acquisition allowed CyberArk to expand its capabilities in the cloud security space and provided Conjur with the resources to scale their solution. The sale of Conjur also allowed Elizabeth and Kevin to create their next company, AppMap, and their next big idea.

Elizabeth Lawler and Kevin Gilpin's career journey is a testament to the power of identifying a market need and developing innovative solutions to meet those needs. It is also a powerful example of how your talents, passions, and skills can propel your career when combined with the right motivation and resources.

Today, Elizabeth and Kevin's life is not stress-free, but their stressors are more controlled, and they have more resources to address them when they arise. And there's been a hidden benefit: Their four children have learned early about the reward and happiness of work by watching their parents lovingly collaborate and have fun doing it. (And yes: their three sons and daughter each have their own "ventures.")

Unfortunately, people like Elizabeth and Kevin are in the minority today. A 2022 study conducted by the American Psychological Association (APA) found that over two-thirds of Americans live with stress. Both money and work are among the leading sources of that stress.[2]

We want you to be on the lower stress side of the continuum. To get you there, we need you to understand an important equation. Your resources, like your time and money, turn into your stressors based on this formula:

resources < demands = stress

Workplace stress is the relationship between the work-related demands on the employee and the amount of control or support that he or she must have to meet the demands. High demands, low control, and low support combine to produce work-related stress.[3]

If you don't have enough time to finish a project, you become stressed. If you don't have enough money to pay your bills, you become stressed. In this chapter, we want you to understand your resources, as Elizabeth and Kevin did, and grow them in a meaningful way without working longer hours just for the sake of greater income.

We don't want anyone to experience work-related stress as we both did earlier in our careers. In both of our cases, we took on more work-related responsibility than the 24-hour-per-day reality would allow. We used time each day that should have been spent with loved ones on an overflow of responsibilities. In both our cases, health and relationships suffered. Hindsight being crystal clear, we can offer advice to prevent this stress. We want you to use your precious resources better than we did. We want you to keep from burning out too soon.

As we'll discuss again in the next chapter, burnout is a serious risk from too much work-related stress. Burnout is generally a function of prolonged exposure to work stress in situations where one lacks control over changing or complex work situations and is unable to see any benefits, even though the effort is there.[4] Burnout would be like trying to run up a never-ending steep hill at the same pace. At some point your body stops your ability to continue. Ongoing exposure to this type of stress is detrimental to your physical and emotional well-being. Anyone who ever feels exhausted after a stressful day of work knows that this is true.

We want you to grow your career without experiencing burnout. To do this, let's first start by understanding two primary resources in the stress equation: time and money. We wish we could create more hours in a day and remove every low-value demand on your time. It would be great if we could add zeroes to your bank account or make student loan debt disappear. We cannot do either of these for you. You can, though. Read on. This chapter focuses on four issues related to the stress equation, particularly the resources of time and money—and how to work them:

1. Myths about career-related stress

2. Protecting and leveraging your time

3. Leveraging your money

4. Other ways to expand and control your resources

Myths about career-related stress

There are three myths associated with work-related stress:

- **Myth 1: Those who are the most successful in their careers are also the most stressed; you cannot have it all.** Although it is true that added responsibilities can be a source of stress, it is also true that those with higher-level and successful entrepreneurial careers tend to have *greater resources* to be effective in those roles and *more control* over how they accomplish their tasks. The extra resources and control translate into lower stress levels, not higher ones.

- **Myth 2: Managing people causes stress.** Yes, people are unpredictable. They have a myriad of dispositional and personal problems that can make managing them a challenge. However, if you select your team well, the people who work for you can lower your work-related stress because they can free your time. Having motivated and talented people working for you is an excellent way to *increase your resources*. You can delegate low-value tasks, giving you *greater control* over your time.

- **Myth 3: Working part-time (or in a low-paying routine job) will reduce work-related stress because there will be no pressure to perform.** Similar to the first misperception, it is generally the case that the lower you are in the organizational chart, the less control you have over how you perform your tasks and how you allocate your time and resources. Unfortunately, those who believe that part-time or more routine work will lower their stress level usually find the opposite to be true. They are under the greatest pressure because they have the *least control* over the work they do and the *fewest available resources*.

As these myths suggest, when control and resources increase, work-related stress levels decline—even in the face of greater responsibilities and demands. We are encouraging you to manage your career with the idea of taking the greatest control you can over the stress equation. This means that as you are increasing your responsibilities, you are concurrently understanding the low-value demands on your time and money. We want you to have greater demands—but the kind that cause positive outcomes for your time and money. Rather than your demands adding negative stress, the additional demands should cause *eustress*, or "good stress." Eustress is associated with excitement, joy, and pride in your accomplishments.

We are not naïve. Some career-related stress will be the bad kind of stress—when you just don't have the time, money, skills, or energy to do what you need to do. This is expected, especially at the start of each new phase when you are building your career within that phase. To keep your negative stress low, we need to discuss the supply-side of this equation: your ability to increase and control your resources. *The last thing we want to do is create more stress in your life without concurrently helping you build the resources side of this equation.*

In the next chapter, we will talk about ways to increase your energy level by improving your physical and emotional well-being. If you improve your well-being overall, your available resources will increase immediately because you will have more energy. Energy is a resource that enables you to move faster, think more clearly, and act more purposefully. By increasing your energy level in a healthy way, you should be able to benefit from a lower overall stress level provided your demands do not increase. Let's discuss two other resources you can marshal, time and money, as you build your career.

Protecting and leveraging your time

People from most well-educated, cosmopolitan cultures view time as a commodity. We spend time. We waste time. We buy time. We make time. Our time is a 24-7 limited resource. As much as we believe we can control time, we are always bound to twenty-four hours in a day. What you do with those twenty-four hours each day will greatly influence the success of your career. We wish we could suggest a way to make a day longer than twenty-four hours, but a professor and an entrepreneur cannot solve time travel. We might be able to help you *find* some time.

Countless books and articles have been written about time management. Over the years, passively or actively, we have been taught numerous time-saving techniques: how to answer emails expeditiously, how to politely cut off long-winded colleagues when they are taking up too much of our time, how to preplan and cook meals so we can save time on dinner preparation, and how to organize our closets to save minutes otherwise wasted on wardrobe indecision every morning. *When did we become so desperate to reclaim time that we need patronizing advice on writing, talking, eating, and dressing ourselves?* Please.

You don't need time-management advice. You need to rethink your relationship with time. You need to fall in love with the twenty-four hours you have each day. You need to love, honor, and respect your time. When you think about it, time is with you until death do you part. You are in a relationship with this twenty-four-hour limited commodity. And even if you thought you and time had a more casual relationship, like it or not you've made a commitment. So, instead of time management advice, we'd like you to think about the kind of advice given in couples therapy. For one week, at the end of each day, write down the two most fulfilling activities of the day and the two most meaningless activities of the day. Estimate the amount of time spent on each. What pattern do you see? Generally, this exercise sheds some light on how well you have been respecting and protecting your time. If there is room for improvement, the following sections discuss a few suggestions for respecting and protecting your time.

TURN OFF YOUR TV AND OTHER DIGITAL DISTRACTIONS

A recent study[5] found that adults in the United States spend about three hours each day watching traditional television and almost three hours on digital media smartphones, social networks, digital video, digital audio, etc. If you do nothing else except turn off your television, you can reclaim enough time to dedicate to a career goal, redirect the time to loved ones, focus on your physical or emotional well-being, and the like. Putting down the phone will also help you reclaim a significant amount of time, and you won't get any pushback from your social media app.

One great strategy is to only watch television when you have a specific show, sporting event, or movie you want to see. For most people, mindless time scrolling through feeds, videos, or channels is *not* time well spent. If you watch or surf or text or do anything blindly, you are not respecting and protecting your vulnerable and valuable time. However, you might have a TV program, video game, or online poker tournament that you view as a meaningful use of time because it is a source of recreation or relaxation.

Ascribing meaning to your activities whether fulfilling or meaningless is your decision. *Who are we to tell you what these activities mean to you?* The point is that you are in control of your day, so it is up to you to make sure you use your twenty-four hours purposefully. Do not blindly turn on your television or pick up your smartphone to scroll during your free time because you have nothing better to do. You have something much better to do with that precious time: Go out and start a new leg of your career journey.

SHED HASSLES AND LOW-PRIORITY TASKS

Another way to respect and protect your time is to reduce the hassles and low-importance tasks. Small changes to the way you manage your errands, such as having your dry cleaning, groceries, and prescriptions delivered, hiring a cleaning person, or setting up your bills to be paid automatically, can save you a great amount of time. Think of the various things in your life that you could automate or outsource.

Paula is an avid user of services like Instacart and Uber. These services have helped her reclaim the time that was spent grocery shopping and commuting, activities she dislikes. If you are a person who finds joy in selecting produce or driving, your strategy to save time would be different from hers. What tasks can you (happily) outsource?

LEVERAGE FLEXIBLE WORK OPPORTUNITIES AND TIME-SAVING BENEFITS

Popularized because of the COVID-19 pandemic, many organizations are allowing people to work from home. This is a good thing. Meta-analyses have found that the greater use of flexible work arrangements, such as the opportunity to work from home a few days each week, leads to employees' better job satisfaction, psychological health,[6] and physical health.[7] If possible, you might want to consider working for an organization that allows some form of flexible work arrangements to give you more control over your time. Likewise, you might want to consider working for an organization offering "family friendly" work/life practices, such as an on-site day care center. These offerings are designed to (and do) increase employees' satisfaction, improve retention, and improve employee performance.[8] These practices have the added benefit of helping you manage your responsibilities while enjoying more time for the things you most want to do (e.g., spend time with your children, practice a hobby, add a starter job for a new career act).

CONCENTRATE INSTEAD OF MULTITASKING

There is plenty of science to support why you should not multitask if multitasking serves as a distraction or uses more cognitive resources than you have available to do two things at once.[9] The reason is that the brain's executive function, your "internal CEO," is designed to provide cognitive resources to one task at a time. When you fragment your attention by trying to do several things at once, you force your brain to reorient to each task each time you shift back to it from whatever else you're doing.

Try this for five minutes: Watch a TV news program that offers both a story on the screen and a series of headlines scrolling at the bottom. *Can you follow both simultaneously?* Most of us believe we can, but, in truth, we cannot. If you had to take a quiz on what you just saw, heard, and read, how well would you do? The participants in numerous studies in cognitive psychology on dichotic listening (listening to multiple things simultaneously) and selective attention (attending and effectively understanding multiple things simultaneously) did not do very well. The fact is that, like it or not, the human brain is limited in how much it can process effectively at one time. Multitasking is, in effect, "exceeding the design specs" of the human brain.

It is very typical to see laptops open in today's college classrooms and students taking notes on the computer versus doing it with pen and paper. We can appreciate this. Trying to take notes while sourcing information or, even worse, online shopping just doesn't work. Students who use laptops often believe they are more efficient when they multitask because they can look up information while the lecture is being presented. In an experimental study, the opposite was found: students who were allowed to use their laptops to multitask during class scored lower on both recall and recognition tests, compared with those who were not allowed to keep their laptops open.[10] The result held regardless of whether their multitasking browsing was related to class material.

Even if the tasks are not simultaneous, we also lose time when we keep many tasks going at a single time, changing rapidly from task to task. Other research[11] found that individuals in their studies lost time when they changed tasks, and the negative effect of time loss was the greatest when trying to change across multiple complex tasks. It is more efficient to focus on one thing at a time. If you opt to spend your precious time on a meaningful activity in your personal or professional life, concentrate on it. Focus.

CONTROL YOUR TIME FOR MULTIPLE CAREER ACTS

If you opt for multiple simultaneous career acts discussed earlier in the book, the result *might be* more time-related stress. As much as possible, try to facilitate a way in which your career acts can sync across your resources. Career acts, when well-coordinated, will not detract from each other. For example, the days off or free time not occupied by one career act should afford you the time for another career act. If you are stressed because of your career acts, you might need to scale back or omit an act.

Many with successful multiple career acts have clear times for when they are working on each career act. For some, it is seasonal. For others, it is weekly or daily. You might have a busy season during which you focus more time on one career act. You might have a career act that you work on during the week and another on the weekends. You might have a career act that you work on during the day and another one that is accomplished in the evening. In your career, be careful not to take on more than what you can manage effectively and successfully. This is particularly important if you have never managed multiple concurrent important roles. Start your multiple-act career slowly. Build it methodically. Stay in control.

FREE YOUR TIME WITH THE HELP OF OTHERS

The people who work for you, whether your cleaning person or your team of direct reports, can free some of your time to focus on your career. Even if you don't have employees working for you, there are a variety of ways the talents of others can help you free some time.

TEMPORARY TASK-BASED ASSISTANCE

The gig economy is growing rapidly. Today many talented people offer their services as freelancers, by the task or job. For example, a bookkeeper might charge for the accounts he handles, such as the number of invoices sent. A customer service professional might charge you only for the service calls she completes. An editor charges you to edit only the documents you send them. Without adding staff, you can add a bookkeeper, a customer service professional, and an editor to shed some of your tasks. "Per diem" professionals are another possible way to free your time.

COMMISSION-BASED ASSISTANCE

Like leveraging the skills of task-based professionals, you can also consider hiring people to sell for you and your business. You pay only for the sales they make, giving the sales representatives a percentage as their commission.

BARTERED ASSISTANCE

This is a time-honored approach to extend your own resources by swapping what you do well (and easily) for what another person does well (and easily). For example, you can offer to cook dinners for your next-door neighbor two nights a week in exchange for her doing the bookkeeping for your small business. It is likely that you were cooking dinner twice a week anyhow and doubling the amount of food to serve two households does not take more of your time.

DIRECT REPORTS

If you are currently working for an organization or are an entrepreneur and have people reporting to you, please remember that having the right people (with the necessary skill set) in the right place (working on useful tasks) at the right time is critical for your ability to perform your own job well. While highly oversimplified, the following are some basic rules of managing people we have found most useful:

1. **Select well.** There is no single more important task than employee selection when it comes to managing your direct reports. People will

bring with them their knowledge, skills, and abilities, but also their motivation and commitment. Select for the skills most necessary for the job. Select for the other attributes affecting the individual's ability to be effective working on your team. Selecting for the appropriate academic degree is more effective than selecting for degrees of separation from Aunt Gladys. ("Yes, Auntie, your neighbor's nephew *is* a wonderful person, but we're not looking for a street mime right now.") We encourage you to involve some of the team members (those with whom the person will work) to participate in the selection process. Whether you are a sole proprietor about to add your first employee or work for a large firm hiring a person to work in your business unit, take this step seriously. The people you hire will have an immediate and direct effect on your own career. They will either decrease your stress level by extending your available resources or (if you choose the wrong individuals) add to your stress in any of a host of ways.

2. **Train effectively.** Once your direct reports have been working for you for a short time, you will have a better sense of their strengths and the areas in which they need development. Think of training as an investment in building necessary knowledge, skills, and abilities among your direct reports. Training is essential and should be thought of as a priority investment into the future of your own career act. Again, think about the ways your direct reports extend your ability to be more effective in your career act, whether working for yourself with one employee or for a larger organization.

3. **Develop and expand roles in meaningful ways.** It is possible, but unlikely, that the job you offer might be your direct report's ideal career act. Remember that those who work for you are aspiring to stimulating and income-generating activities just as you are. When thinking about your direct reports, you might want to consider how the job you offer fits into the scheme of their individual career

acts. Even if you cannot offer what is most fulfilling to them, you might want to talk about how they would like to develop their careers to become more motivating in the future. Understanding a person's key motivators will unlock their potential and extend you in wonderful ways.

4. **Show appreciation**. There are perhaps no two more powerful words for motivating your direct reports than the words "thank you." When you say the words, be sure they are meaningful and sincere, matching the behaviors you would like to see repeated. The common advice to "catch them doing something right" and express your appreciation on the spot is extremely wise, and not followed often enough. There is no faster way to douse your employees' fire of energy than to underappreciate them.

Protecting and leveraging your money

How much money do you need to achieve your ideal career goal? The answer, of course, depends on the nature of your ideal career and whether it will require an investment in education, materials, equipment, and the like. To become a physician, for example, the education might cost hundreds of thousands of dollars. At the other end of the scale, selling your watercolor paintings might have a lower start-up cost (unless you choose to go to medical school first.)

You need to ask yourself: *What are the financial investments I will need to make to achieve my ideal career?* There is some truth in the cliché: "You need to spend money to make money." Please don't let the price tag of your ideal career hold you back. Instead, be realistic about your goals and their costs and make certain they are worthy of your financial investment. Think through the next exercise to try to estimate the costs of one of your chosen career acts.

FUNDING A CAREER ACT

The truth is that great careers almost always require some financial invest-ment. Although being frugal and saving money is usually good, no one has ever saved their way to prosperity. The following are some useful exercises to consider with respect to the money you will need for a chosen career.

1. **Talk to several people who are currently in your ideal career.** Ask them to describe the investments they made along the way in terms of education, training, equipment, certificates, licensures, office space, systems, and the like. Ask each person, "What do you believe was the best investment you made in your career?" Be sure to ask more than one person, so that you can see if there are consis-tent themes among people who are successful in the career you are contemplating. You can also research the cost of your ideal career from reputable sources, such as professional or trade associations. If you are relying only on interviews, understand that requirements for your career act might have changed since your interviewees were first beginning their careers, so you might need *to add some items to your initial funding list*.

2. **Create a goal for the total amount of money you believe you will need.** Review your funding list and research what those invest-ments in your career would cost in today's dollars. What is your funding total? Now, add 20 percent (or more) to the total. This is your new required *funding total* for your career act. Although 20 percent may seem like a lot, we know that there are always unex-pected expenses along the way. If that number seems very high to you, review the money strategies earlier in this chapter. Plus, we can't think of anyone who was overly stressed because they saved more than they spent for a goal.

3. **Determine ways to fund the career act.** Whatever the total funding amount required, *you should have a realistic plan for ways to raise*

the money needed. You have three options to raise that money: save money, earn it, or borrow it.

You might have a total amount in mind—and even a plan to get there. This is great. At this stage, we'd like you to consider three more issues than just "how to" fund. Working them through early can help prevent more angst down the road.

1. **How much income can you realistically anticipate generating from this career act, and how soon?** This is especially true for career acts requiring a major investment, such as years of education and training, or a large lump-sum initial expense in starting a new business. For example, there has been a shortage of nurses, which is expected to continue past 2025 as the population ages and requires more medical care.[12] If you complete nursing school, you can be almost guaranteed a financially rewarding full-time job as soon as you pass the licensure examination to become an RN. On the other hand, if you return to school for a master's degree in art history with a specialization on Ming dynasty Chinese ceramics, you might need a longer time frame to find an ideal career.

2. **What is your comfort level with debt?** Some people are optimistic to the point of almost being reckless with money, whereas others need to be reminded that it's financially wise to spend some money to invest in your career to make more money long term.

3. **If you are in a committed relationship, is your spouse or partner able to support the funding of this career act, as an investment in your family?** In many cases, a spouse or partner works full-time and earns enough to support the couple while the other spouse or partner starts a new career act. Sometimes couples will take turns working at full-time jobs until they both attain the careers they enjoy. Couples might also agree to scale back their collective expenses temporarily while investing in careers.

PROTECT YOUR MONEY

Investing in your career could be easier than you think if you already have some discretionary income. If you are in this situation, you can think of ways to reduce spending without drastically changing your lifestyle. Discretionary income is the amount remaining from your income after you have paid your taxes, insurance, rent/mortgage, and all other life essentials, such as your housing, food, transportation, and clothing. Can you reinvest some of this money in yourself? The answer is probably yes.

If you don't have any discretionary income at this time, you might want to think about the ways you are spending money. Can you "find" money in places and reallocate it to career-related investments? Rooting through the couch cushions isn't what we had in mind. Here are some ways you might be able to locate money:

1. Do you buy items that you could easily borrow, like books from a library or tools from a neighbor? Thanks to technology and a plethora of apps, there are many new ways to find a shareable asset that you can use short-term, instead of buying.

2. Do you buy clothes you don't wear? When Paula was starting her career, a helpful exercise for her was to calculate the number of times she wore an item of clothing relative to its price. She calculated the price of the outfit she was wearing as she walked out the door, it being less expensive with each wear. Hardly obsessive (she still likes nice clothes), this exercise did help her curb her shopping habit.

3. Do you have subscriptions or memberships you don't use (e.g., apps, streaming services, gym)? The question for each is whether you would miss it if you didn't have it.

4. Do you have items in your refrigerator that you don't use before they expire? An easy way to reshape this is to take the food you are about to throw away and put the same amount of money in the trash. (OK, reclaim the money out of the garbage. No one should throw away

money. And it is healthier than forcing yourself to eat expired foods to justify buying them.) If you do this exercise enough times, this might change your behavior.

Before you clip and cut your way through your expenses, though, think through their implications for your career. For example, giving up your cleaning person might be a way to save money, but the hours you can invest in yourself by having someone else clean your house might be worth the investment. Buying a beautiful interview suit is worth every penny if you get the dream job for which a great suit was needed. Skipping this year's trade show might also save money, but the loss of potential contacts and ideas might be the wrong item to cut from your budget. You see the pattern. Saving toward building your career is different from cutting extras that are not immediately needed. Only you can determine where and how you can most wisely save and spend the money you need.

Expensive degree programs and entrepreneurial ventures aside (they are likely to be a more serious investment of money), here are few low-cost ways to add to the investment into your career:

1. Take a class, seminar, or e-learning course. Many public libraries offer access to online learning courses for free. Free is good.

2. Attend a networking event, seminar, or trade show.

3. Buy necessary computer equipment, data storage, software, applications, memberships, data subscriptions, or other tools-of-the-trade.

4. Buy professional resources to enhance your blog, podcast, professional social media presence, or personal brand.

5. Hire a person to help you with household chores or other nonwork tasks to free up more of your time.

6. Identify those who might be able to give you career guidance and treat them to lunch, dinner, a drink, or a coffee.

As we mentioned at the start of this chapter, there is no magic available to effortlessly and immediately grow the hours in a day or your financial resources. But we hope we have given you some tips for how to protect and effectively leverage the time and money you have so you can move closer to your career goals.

KEY TAKEAWAYS

- Do you erroneously believe the myths of career-related stress? Review the list in this chapter to gain some self-awareness.

- Protect and leverage your time by turning off your TV and other digital distractions, shedding hassles and low-priority tasks, using the flexible work options and timesaving benefits you are offered, and avoiding (or being thoughtful about) multitasking.

- Consider freeing more of your time by engaging people for temporary-task-based, commission-based, and bartered assistance.

- Manage the talented people who are helping you achieve your work goals by selecting well, training and motivating effectively, and appreciating the role they are playing in your success.

- Understand that your career will likely require some financial investment. Be realistic about this investment by talking to others about the career to which you aspire and doing your homework. Review and exhaust all funding options.

- Protect your money and invest savings into your career. Determine where and how you can most wisely save and spend the money you need.

CHAPTER 9

INCREASE YOUR PHYSICAL AND EMOTIONAL WELL-BEING

The first requisite of success is the ability to apply your physical and mental energies to one problem without growing weary.

—THOMAS EDISON

On paper, Bill Drayton reads like a Hollywood version of an American success story: a bachelor's degree from Harvard, a master's in economics from Balliol College at Oxford University, a JD from Yale University Law School, and working for McKinsey & Company in New York by age twenty-seven.[1] From 1977 to 1981 he served as an assistant administrator at the US Environmental Protection Agency, where he launched emissions trading (the basis of the Kyoto Protocol) and other reforms.

Then he went off script (ours, not his). The next natural move by the hero in our movie might have been to seek an even higher government position or a lucrative CEO slot, or maybe start his own company in the private sector.

Instead, in 1980, he founded *Ashoka: Innovators for the Public*, a 501(c) corporation to help support, connect, and build up entrepreneurs and their ideas for correcting entrenched global problems. Drayton had observed that there is nothing more powerful than an entrepreneur with a big idea. He founded Ashoka while he worked part-time at McKinsey. With the support that he received when elected a MacArthur Fellow (more popularly known as a "Genius Grant") in 1984, he was able to devote himself fully to Ashoka.

By leading Ashoka, Drayton pioneered the new field. The organization grew a global association of over four thousand leading social entrepreneurs in ninety-three countries worldwide, who today work together to identify intractable social problems, have great ideas to fix them, and engage teams to help. Ashoka supports these social entrepreneurs, called "Ashoka Fellows," with grants to support their launches.

There is more to Bill Drayton's backstory. Although he is credited for coining the term "social entrepreneurship" in 1972, he acknowledges that this is a concept that has been around for centuries. In his own life, he was a social entrepreneur long before the term was coined. For example, in the fall of 1961 he launched several organizations, including Harvard's Ashoka Table, an interdisciplinary weekly forum in the social sciences. The goal of Ashoka Table was to look at how society functioned. After that, he founded Yale Legislative Services (YLS), a Yale Law School student-managed program that engaged one-third of the law school students in helping craft legislation across the Northeast. Proposed projects often came from legislators, public interest groups, and government organizations. Services were provided at no charge.

The spark that ignited him had happened in 1961, when he and several of his fellow rising college sophomores had an opportunity to visit India. Drayton had long been inspired by India's civilization and culture—and motivated by India's approach to civil rights. In India, he and his friends found friendly, energetic, and entrepreneurial people on every street corner. How could this energy and intellect be used to overcome social challenges, one problem at a time? Drayton wondered. Moreover, what could a bunch of sophomores do? Finding these answers and harnessing their potential propelled his purpose-driven career.

Fast forward to today, Drayton deeply appreciates that we're living in a world where artificial intelligence and machines now do much of what people once did for employment, whether the work was in fields, factories, or offices. The work has changed. The workers' skills have changed, and the world of employment has changed. Companies want to hire people who can see problems and foster change, not just follow rules using repetitive skills. He understands that the world needs changemakers to do what technology cannot.

Returning to his perceptions in India, the motivation behind changemaking needs to start with young people, Drayton believes. In fact, he suggested back in 2018 that we need another kind of "literacy"—a "changemaker literacy" that parents and educators should be fostering in children. "Changemaking is the new literacy. It is the new reality," Drayton says today.

From this deep philosophy to empower change, Ashoka unveiled its ambitious vision, "Everyone a Changemaker" (called EACH), back in 2005. Ashoka's vision for EACH is: ". . . that because we are living in a truly historic moment where anyone can create positive change; everyone needs to become a changemaker in order to thrive; and everyone should be equipped with the qualities that most define a social entrepreneur."[2]

That starts with the right to give, a basic human right that's often challenged because of social, economic, educational, gender, age, and other disparities, which (at least on the surface) may reduce the power to effect real change. Such inequality may discourage or prevent people from taking action to solve pressing problems that they see around them. As its Fellows have demonstrated, Ashoka knows how to fix this.

In 2023, about a third of Ashoka Fellows lead social entrepreneurship programs focused on kids, with about 87 percent of them putting kids in charge in hundreds of different ways. Participants come from disadvantaged backgrounds and in about a million schools around the world. "And it works," he says. "If you give kids an opportunity to be givers, they intuitively know that's the key. They want to be givers and be powerful. And once you've done that, you know that the world is going to want you."

Looking ahead, Ashoka is identifying emerging opportunities where society is reaching a tipping point that will make it possible to solve critical problems through widespread systemic change. It does this by helping entrepreneurs work with each other, and with partners in business, government, academia, and other influential institutions to draw on and demonstrate the power of collaborative entrepreneurship.

Not surprisingly, Drayton has received numerous awards and accolades over the decades since he went "off script" and founded Ashoka. He has produced a positive ripple in the world and is helping to be part of the solution.

If we only look at the outcomes, it can be easy to forget the physical and emotional energy behind Drayton's success. From the early 1960s, when he had the opportunity to admire the energy and entrepreneurship pulsing through India, he knew that having a purpose was energy-enhancing. At the same time, he also recognized that people do not have a limitless supply of resources. Physical and emotional energy needs to be harnessed in a way that actions have the greatest chance to be successful and endure.

Drayton believes that you should, first, do what you love that aligns with your inner purpose and talents. Second, have some patience to give opportunities a chance to form, launch, and grow. Toiling where you are not engaged saps physical and emotional energy. Planting a garden before it has been prepared is also a waste of physical and emotional resources.

As for his own work, Drayton observes: "Good physical and emotional well-being are a direct function of being a changemaker and of being able to give others the gift of giving. The right to give is the most fundamental right. Being a giver makes you healthy and want to be healthy because it is so much fun and satisfying. It's multiplicative." For his part, Drayton neither smokes nor drinks, watches himself around brownies (his favorite sweet), and backpack-hikes regularly, including an annual contemplative, three-week backpacking trip into the wilderness.

So much of this book focused on harnessing and developing your talents toward your ultimate career goal. This chapter is different. We want to expand your physical and emotional resources with tips and tools, so you have the energy to work toward the goals you set. These tips and tools are neither exhaustive nor comprehensive—and they are not intended to replace advice from your healthcare provider or mental health professional. We are not physicians, clinical or counseling psychologists, personal trainers, sleep experts, nutritionists, etc. The advice, tools, and suggested books in this section are for illustration and offered from our personal experiences, what has worked for one (or both) of us. Please do not make changes without consulting your healthcare professionals.

Physical and emotional well-being

A positive career journey requires increased physical stamina and emotional strength. You will use greater task-focused effort, more emotional bandwidth, and a higher level of mental energy to engage your body and mind. Raw motivation to move your career in exciting directions isn't enough. You need to fill the tanks, so to speak, to take care of your physical and emotional resources. Ignoring these precious resources ends up taking a toll. You'll run out of gas. Both of us, early in our careers, learned this lesson the hard way, thankfully before any permanent damage or burnout could set in.

In 1997, Paula was thirty years old and couldn't ignore the growing beat of her looming tenure clock. Her tenure case at Rutgers University would go forward in 2001 but the research she was conducting at the time would have make-or-break consequences on her case. At that same time, her consulting and speaking engagements were starting to increase. She had stopped all exercise (who had time for exercise?), worked until late on several consecutive nights each week (who had time for sleep?), ate fast food (who had time to cook?), and had a work-related social life (who had time to meet new people?). You can predict what happened next, right? Her health declined to the point where she ended up with a long series of medical tests for unexplained concerning symptoms—along with more than a few relationships that went sideways. Thankfully, one of the doctors she was seeing took the time to provide the wisdom she needed to hear: "if you don't manage the stress in your life, it will continue to erode your health." Some of the changes she tried to make lasted the length of the typical New Year's resolution—a few weeks. Others did stick. She started sleeping more, joined a painting class to decompress, and hired a trainer. The scheduling of wellness-related activities helped her back then—and continues to help her today.

Andy also had the experience in which pushing himself too hard had a negative effect on his well-being. After building pcOrder.com, a company in Austin, Texas, that he took public in 1997, he found himself in a state of clinical depression. One of his mentors at the time, Frank Moss, was incredible throughout the process. Frank told Andy and his wife at the time that they shouldn't worry about work and to just get healthy. And not worry if it took three weeks, three months, or three years: that he was there, supportive of Andy getting back on his feet and as healthy as possible. Andy notes that "it was truly remarkable to have such incredible unconditional support from one's coworkers and, in this case, a close friend and trusted mentor." He took some time and reclaimed his health.

Learn from our mistakes. Doing what you love is stimulating and fulfilling; however, if you embed more work-related activities into an overly stressed, anxiety-filled, or low-energy lifestyle, you will be setting yourself up for great personal frustration, a lower quality of life, poor health, or possibly burnout. And how much will you be able to enjoy your fulfilling career if it means never seeing the sun, living on potato chips, and sleeping on the office floor? We want the best for you, in your career and your life.

Before planning and growing your career, look inward. *Are you physically and emotionally ready for a more engaging career, one that will likely require a higher level of personal resources?* If you are like many, including us, the answer is probably "not yet." A study[3] by the World Health Organization (WHO) estimated that nearly 28 percent of adults in the world, about 1.5 billion people, do not get enough weekly exercise (i.e., 75 minutes of vigorous exercise or 150 minutes of moderate-intensity exercise). Globally, nearly 1 billion people have a mental health or substance abuse disorder,[4] a statistic estimated prior to the pandemic. These statistics present the extremes but serve as a reminder that many people can benefit from a renewed commitment to improve our physical and mental well-being.

A meta-analysis of almost five hundred studies[5] found positive relationships between job satisfaction and many indicators of health, both physical and psychological well-being. In a large-scale study across many countries, the ability to effectively integrate one's work and nonwork life was positively related to both job satisfaction and life satisfaction and negatively related to anxiety and depression.[6] To *live for a living*, we want you to have a fulfilling career without sacrificing your physical health and emotional well-being. We want you to get the most from your career and your life.

SHARE YOUR WELLNESS TIPS AND SUCCESSES

In this chapter, we shared our favorite pieces of advice, tools, and books with you. Now, we'd like you to share the same with us. Please share any resources you found effective and your success stories in increasing your physical and emotional well-being.

We and the entire "Live for a Living" community would love to learn from you. Remember to add #LiveforaLiving.

Strategies to improve your well-being

You can increase your physical and emotional well-being in many ways. Since many roads will lead to the same destination, this section is designed to offer a general direction but not a GPS for wellness. We encourage you to listen to your body and your healthcare provider to determine the best way forward. The advice we offer is high-level, such as "spend time in nature" and not specific. Everyone is different. As an example, Andy is an athlete who played rugby for many years. His wellness plan includes challenging endurance hikes for both exercise and a boost of endorphins. Paula can achieve the same wellness goal as Andy without much risk of twisting an ankle. She prefers taking ten thousand steps in a well-manicured park to Andy's preference for scaling the side of a steep cliff. We have the same goal (spend time in nature) with different approaches (ankle twisting for Andy versus comfort for Paula). You are unique. Make these goals your own so they more naturally become part of your life.

SOME OF OUR FAVORITE MIND-BODY BOOKS

- *Why We Sleep* by Matthew Walker
- *Better than Before* by Gretchen Rubin
- *10% Happier* by Dan Harris
- *Didn't See It Coming* by Cary Nieuwhof
- *The Happiness Hypothesis* by Jonathan Haidt
- *The Four Agreements* by don Miguel Ruiz
- *The How of Happiness* by Sonja Lyubomirsky
- *Essentialism* by Greg McKeown
- *Atomic Habits* by James Clear
- *Feeling Good* by David Burns

EAT WELL

Nutritional advice abounds for ways to maintain a healthy diet. Most of these expert suggestions converge around the following pieces of advice:

- Eat fiber-filled whole foods, such as fruit, raw vegetables, nuts, and seeds.

- Eat foods that are higher in lean protein and healthy unsaturated fats (foods such as avocados, salmon, chicken, and legumes).

- Drink water instead of fruit juices, soda, or sports drinks.

- Limit your sodium intake to about 2,300 mg per day.

- Limit your sugar intake to fewer than 10% of your daily calorie intake.

- Avoid processed foods, especially those with saturated fats, high-fructose corn syrup, artificial sweeteners, and preservatives.

- Eat whole foods you can pronounce, recognize, and even draw (if you are artistic).

- If you consume alcohol, do so in moderation (which is generally much lower than most people think).

- Avoid calorie-restrictive diets that leave you hungry and without energy (better to eat healthy food combined with exercise).

Remember, just because someone was thoughtful enough to leave donuts in the break room doesn't mean you have to take one. You can do a web search relatively easily on sites such as the Mayo Clinic, CDC, or the American Heart Association to receive more than enough advice on eating well. As always, check with your healthcare provider before altering your diet. Don't take our word for it. Consult the professionals as we both did.

With respect to how and when to eat, the advice seems to change quickly. As we are writing this book, intermittent fasting or time-limited eating seems to be showing limited success for some people. As an example of when you should listen to your body and your healthcare provider, intermittent fasting doesn't work for Paula, who is more energetic when starting the day with a high-protein breakfast, usually eggs and veggies—with coffee, lots of coffee. She eats small, healthy snacks (fruit and nuts) throughout the day, the exact opposite of intermittent fasting.

Andy has a different approach. As a diabetic, he must eat a high-protein, low-carb diet, and has, in consultation with his doctor, gone back and forth trying various diets to get there. He, like most people, reverts to comfort foods and some bad habits when stressed. Over time, he has balanced the times when he is nutritionally "well-behaved" with the times when he "cuts himself a break," usually when under extreme stress. He drinks Diet Coke on occasion and indulges in some carbs. He has found that giving himself a break makes it easier to sustain a better diet in the long term. The key message: you don't have to be perfect all the time. Being kind to yourself sometimes means cutting yourself some slack and indulging. Maybe . . . half a donut from the break room. And, of course, talk to your doctor.

It is worth mentioning that many of the people profiled in this book eat organic and locally grown food. They have a healthy relationship with food and are careful about what foods they put into their bodies. Many are also "foodies," people who love to cook for themselves and appreciate the quality of the ingredients used by the recipes they frequent. In fairness, those profiled in this book also have the financial resources often associated with these higher-quality foods. In a positive, virtuous cycle, your more rewarding career might encourage an investment back into yourself with respect to the quality of foods you eat.

EXERCISE MORE

The scientific evidence extolling the benefits of exercise is pervasive. We know that any activity that gets our bodies moving is helpful to our health, energy, and stamina in some way. Even a low level of activity, such as getting out of your chair every fifteen minutes when sitting at your desk, can help improve wellness. Aerobic exercise improves stamina and helps reduce feelings of mild depression and anxiety. It releases endorphins and gives us a natural high. Strength training and overall fitness increases our metabolism and physical health. Like a fulfilling career, these are good things. *What do you enjoy that will get you moving?*

To stay committed to physical fitness, try to find some activity that you can share with your partner, coworker, or friend, such as taking brisk walks, playing tennis, or joining a salsa dance class. If you prefer to exercise alone, think about listening to music you find motivating and stimulating. The positive benefits of music are very helpful. If you have a completely sedentary life, start your exercise regimen with manageable physical activities and, again, speak with your healthcare provider before starting a new fitness approach. Here are the most frequent pieces of advice around exercise that one or both of us has adopted:

- It is better to exercise consistently, throughout the day or the week, instead of trying to do a lot of exercise one time (and give up because you couldn't move the next day, you didn't see immediate results, or it was too time-consuming).

- Schedule your exercise or plan to meet a friend to workout. Both will escalate commitment to the exercise, especially your friend who will be waiting for you.

- Aim for at least 150 minutes of moderate exercise every week. Higher intensity is better if you are able.

- Walking is a great form of exercise. Try for a daily hour-long brisk walk of 7,000 to 10,000 steps.

- Be sure to hydrate. Our bodies need water to work effectively.

- Warm up and cool down to avoid injury.

- Do interval training, where you increase the cardio intensity for short periods of time throughout the duration of your workout.

- Do weight-bearing exercise to build muscle mass which increases your capacity to burn calories.

- Make it easy for exercise to become a habit. For example, leave your exercise clothes near your bed so you can easily wear or pack them when you wake up. Even though it might make it even easier, we don't encourage sleeping in your exercise clothes.

- Pair the exercise with something you enjoy, such as watching your favorite show on the treadmill or chatting with a friend during a walk.

Whatever exercise activity you enjoy (and is approved by your health-care provider) is the one that you should do. Paula does not play sports (or even watch sports for that matter) and is not particularly athletic. Finding an "enjoyable exercise" seemed like an oxymoron to her and scheduling work-outs with friends just seemed like another logistical task (no thanks). Except for paddleboarding on a calm lake or easy walks in the forest, neither of which feel like exercise to her, most of her exercise habits are structured activities she can put on her calendar, including sessions with a personal trainer, classes (usually yoga or Pilates), and even walks (alone) with a great podcast.

Andy is very different from Paula. As an athlete and former rugby player, he loves things that involve teams or competition, even though he doesn't play rugby too much anymore. Today, running stairs at Harvard Stadium across the street from where he lives or taking a competitive spinning class meets his needs.

It follows (and, again, might not surprise you) that, among those peo-ple profiled in this book, there are many with personal trainers and home gyms, many who are triathletes, marathon runners, and many who take active vacations such as riding bikes through Tuscany, white-water rafting in Colorado, and trips to climb Mount Kilimanjaro. Because they have great careers, they have the time and the money to engage in these activities. Their energy levels and physical fitness makes them healthy and happy with their career acts. They enjoy the virtuous cycle that we want you to experience as well. We want you to *live for a living*. It is attainable but you need to start the cycle to have one.

GET ENOUGH HIGH-QUALITY SLEEP

The Center for Disease Control's National Center for Chronic Disease Prevention and Health Promotion released a report estimating that 50 to 70 million Americans suffer from chronic sleep loss and sleep disorders. Sleep researchers, such as Dr. Matthew Walker, author of the excellent book *Why We Sleep*, have highlighted the many reasons to get about eight hours of high-quality sleep. A review article[7] reports that sleep deficiency is associated with cognitive problems in concentration and memory, with health problems such as obesity, depression, diabetes, cardiovascular health, immunity, renal function, and respiratory physiology.

How many hours of sleep do you average each night? According to the National Sleep Foundation, most adults need between seven and nine consecutive hours of sleep each night to feel fully rested. *Are you close to getting the sleep you need?* If not, here are some changes that worked for one or both of us:

- Go to bed at the same time every day to get your body into a regular sleep pattern.

- Avoid stimulants such as coffee, tea, and other caffeinated beverages after noon—and be aware that "decaffeinated" coffee still contains some caffeine.

- Try to clear your mind before you go to bed; if you tend to lie awake in bed thinking of things you need to do the next day, write them down before "lights out" and do some meditation deep breathing exercises.

- If reading helps you relax before sleep, limit the time so you don't become engrossed, staying up later than you planned.

- Dim your lights and reduce your exposure to blue light from tablets, smartphones, and all other devices.

- Make sure your bedroom is dark. Detectable light sources will simulate sunlight's cue that it is time to wake up.

- Try to avoid using your bed for non-sleep activities like paying bills, sending emails, or phone conversations. That said, we happily acknowledge that some bedroom-related non-sleep activities are more than acceptable and, in fact, are great for your well-being (and better sleep).

Paula is a self-proclaimed sleep diva, an avid fan of wearing eyeshades, cooling the bedroom to 65 degrees, using a weighted blanket, dimming the room with amber lights before bedtime, taking magnesium a few hours before bedtime, and making sure her partner stays on his side of the bed, especially during those critical hours of deep sleep at the start of the sleep cycle. At the time of this writing, her Oura ring[8] stats put her sleep average at 7 hours and 53 minutes. Not bad. Andy is also an Oura user, with an average sleep of six to eight hours per night. He has found Oura immensely helpful in understanding which patterns of behavior reinforce a solid night's sleep. Most often his sleep is influenced by his caffeine intake. When he takes in less caffeine and gets more exercise, he sleeps better and can deal with stress more effectively.

LAUGH MORE

Do you remember the last time you laughed so hard you cried? Do you remember the feeling immediately after that hearty laugh? It was a natural high, a burst of positive energy, a wonderful buzz. Research has found that laughter provides beneficial health effects for wellness and the boost lasts hours after the laughter subsides.[9] Endorphins are neurotransmitters found in the brain that act as the body's own morphine and that also influence physiological states, such as our feelings of euphoria and a reduction of pain. Laughter has been found to improve your mood, ease stress and tension, and improve our immune systems longer term.[10] When building the foundation for your career, these are all benefits.

In addition to the physical benefits, laughter is also a way to deepen and strengthen bonds between people.[11] As humans we start to laugh when we are about three months old and, if we are fortunate, continue to laugh throughout our lives. Laughter serves as a social glue connecting us to each other. In fact, laughter is a more social activity than most realize. When we watch or experience something funny, we are more likely to laugh if we are with another person than alone. If you can enjoy the laughter with friends and loved ones, even better: this wellness-enhancing experience is heightened when shared.

A few tips for increasing the laughter in your life that works for one or both of us:

1. With TikTok and YouTube providing an endless stream of content for whatever your sense of humor, you won't need to look far to find something that will make you laugh.

2. Find friends who share your sense of humor and make you laugh. Spend more time with them.

3. Remember that humor is person-specific and not (at all) universal. What some people find humorous, others find offensive. (This partially explains the proliferation of funny animal videos, which rarely offend anyone.)

4. Lighten up. Having a fulfilling career does not mean you should give up on laughter.

VOLUNTEER

In addition to laughing, you can also get this natural healthy energy-producing buzz in other ways. Either volunteering your time to a worthy cause (walking dogs for your local animal shelter) or offering a simple act of kindness (helping an elderly person carry his or her groceries) can produce positive health benefits.[12] Think about how you feel when you do nice things for others, especially strangers. You feel good, warm, and fuzzy inside. Psychologists call this feeling the "helper's high." When you are doing nice things for others and feel the helper's high, endorphins are released, resulting in positive physical and emotional health benefits. You can channel the euphoria and energy you feel to benefit your life in many ways, such as giving you more energy for your career.

Volunteering, in addition to being of service to others, has an additional benefit for your career. Many volunteer opportunities can, in fact, be starter career acts, giving you the coveted "triple win": First, society benefits from having your time and talents applied for a greater good, in service to others. Second, your health and energy level improve from the helper's high you feel from the selflessness you show. And third, your career improves from the opportunity to increase your knowledge, skills, and abilities using experiential learning. This might be especially important during the starter career act phase. Research has found that students, for example, acquire soft skills when they volunteer,[13] building professional skills without direct work experience.

If you are thinking about volunteering, select your volunteerism opportunity carefully since your time is a fixed commodity. Think about where you can best apply your natural gifts and talents to maximize the benefit to the recipients and increase your helper's high. It is OK that you combine volunteerism with your passions or interests. It's also OK that your volunteerism provides an opportunity to practice a skill, gain knowledge and experience, and improve your abilities.

ENGAGE IN MINDFULNESS AND MEDITATION

Mindfulness is being fully present in the moment, aware of your thoughts, feelings, and body's sensations. It is an important skill for you to have because people with a higher level of mindfulness are more open to new experiences, such as embarking on a new career act. Mindfulness is a skill and can be learned. It can be practiced almost anywhere, anytime. For example, wherever you are now, spend a moment to sense your thoughts, feelings, and body's sensations without judging them. If you are eating or drinking, actively process the taste, smell, and texture. Be fully aware of your surroundings including the sights, sounds, and smells.

Another way to build your mindfulness is through meditation, as those who meditate experience higher levels of clarity, calm, stability, and concentration as they can stay focused in the present moment.[14] Most meditation practices achieve this by engaging a concentration activity such as focusing on one's breath. The organization Mindful offers five important reasons to meditate: (1) understand your physical and emotional pain points, (2) lower your level of experienced stress, (3) connect better to others and yourself, (4) improve your focus and concentration, and (5) reduce brain chatter and distraction.

There are some popular apps, such as Headspace and Calm, to get you started. Paula uses Muse, a device you can wear as a headband during a meditation session to provide biofeedback on brain waves. Andy prefers yoga as his form of meditation. Shavasana is his happy place.

TAKE A VACATION, STAYCATION, TECH-HOLIDAY

Many of us cite career-related reasons to forgo our vacations: "I'm too busy and will have too much work when I return." "I'm too critical to fully unplug from work." "I am worried about being 'out of touch.'" "I know that Fred from Accounting has been coveting my desk chair and will take it when I'm away." Do any of these sound familiar? Although it is true that there are better and worse times to take vacations, you might be doing more harm to your career by not taking time off to recharge your batteries.

Vacations lasting one week or more have been shown to increase work performance and productivity and have been shown to improve creativity and engagement. A study conducted by Air New Zealand in conjunction with former NASA scientists found[15] that individuals' post-vacation performance improved nearly 25 percent compared with performance before vacation. The results were even more pronounced for those who likely occupy more senior positions, people forty-five years of age and older, demonstrating a 50-percent increase in their post-vacation performance.

To maintain peak performance, increase creativity, and improve mental health and physical well-being, vacations are important, even if the effects do not last forever. One study found that employees reported better health and wellness even during short vacations, lasting four or five days, especially when they could fully relax and detach from work during their time off.[16]

In today's generally overcharged, overly available, ever-changing, and understaffed organizations, employees run the risk of prolonged exposure to stressful work environments—otherwise known as the recipe for burnout. Working from home has made it even more challenging to disengage from our work and work-associated sites. Email, Slack, and the like are just so easy to check, anywhere and anytime. Given that the ill effects of burnout can be permanent, even the most career-minded individuals should consider reaching for the sunblock and trading in some frequent flyer miles if circumstances allow. Or an unplugged, tech-free vacation at home would work too if you don't fill the days with home projects and errands.

Many companies, realizing the downside of prolonged periods of non-stop work, are encouraging employees to use their vacations by creating *disincentives* to skip vacation—limiting the amount of pay for unused vacation days, limiting the number of days that can be carried over to the next year, rewarding supervisors for encouraging vacations, and the like. Great organizations and great leaders know the positive benefits of employees' vacations.

You are probably not too busy to take a vacation, staycation, or a technology-free holiday. However, you might need to plan your vacation to minimize work-related disruptions. For example:

- Many jobs go through annual demand cycles: accountants during tax time, tuxedo renters during wedding season, teachers at the start of the semester, and so on. Try to synchronize your vacations to your organization's business cycle and plan a vacation during an anticipated lighter-workload period.

- Try to find a coworker to take over the most critical tasks for you so you do not return to an organizational crisis. Give your contact information to your designee so that he or she can contact you if a real work-related emergency arises.

- Discuss ahead of time what a real emergency is and what can wait, especially if your designee is someone more junior. "Where do we keep filters for the company coffee machine?" doesn't qualify as a good reason to interrupt your mountaintop holiday.

- You might want to lock your smartphone in the hotel safe during the day (if you can). One person we know gets a "burner phone" for their vacations so they can follow the Red Sox and use the GPS to find their way to the beach without getting any calls from work.

- If you are in a very critical role in your organization, being *minimally* connected while on vacation can help reduce your anxiety and any possible feelings of guilt for relaxing while others work.

- Although the positive effects of vacations are generally associated with longer vacations (at least one week), mini-vacations will help you decompress.

- Keep the positive in mind if you are in a leadership position: Your minimally tethered absence is a great way to develop those you supervise, increasing their capability to handle tasks and decisions independently.

Do you believe that your organization cannot survive without you? You might be right if (and only if) you are a sole proprietor who needs to engage in work every day to generate revenue and cannot close your operation for a period (e.g., you are the only baker in your bakery and you need to supply your only client every day with baked goods or lose the business). Being "truly indispensable" for a limited period while you vacation has a high bar to be credible. Most people can disengage or close for a week without overly negative consequences.

At Tamr, Andy, as the CEO and co-founder, always emphasizes that "the company is bigger than any one person"—including him. If you're a great founder and entrepreneur, you desire to build an organization that can outlast you and doesn't depend on you for survival. Andy is a huge proponent of founder-led companies. Many of the companies he has funded or founded through Koa Labs (Andy's fund for helping start-ups) have a core principle: the best companies (such as Apple, Microsoft, and Amazon) have been founder-led, often for many decades. We believe in this principle. Most of the founders of those companies work hard to build organizations that could continue to be wildly successful even if they as individuals were to disappear.

If you are being conscientious and are sincerely more concerned about your organization's health over your own, perhaps you should rethink the functional role of vacations in productivity. From a purely competitive perspective, the most critical people in organizations are the very people who tend to be most susceptible to burnout because they seek high-responsibility positions, tend to personalize work, and tend to weave their careers deeply into their self-identity. If this describes you, then a vacation, when well-timed and well-planned, will help *improve* your work performance. Perhaps your more honest psychological concern is that the organization will do just fine without you. If this is the case, look within yourself and build some professional self-confidence.

Vacations and performance excellence are not mutually exclusive. The more enlightened organizations know this and know that their best performers will burn out if they forsake the wellness-enhancing benefits of vacations. At Tamr, Andy and his company have a policy that enables everyone to determine their need for vacation. This is challenging because each individual needs to develop the skills to determine when to take time off to maintain personal balance. We believe that self-determination of work/life balance is unique to every individual: each person has a unique amount of ambition and need for time off. Having a policy that enables each person to find their own balance (within reason) is something that, if learned at a young age, becomes a core skill that can be brought to any organization, regardless of its potentially outdated, post-industrial vacation policies. It's hard to figure out how to manage your own work/life harmony within the context of your professional ambitions. However, the earlier you figure it out in your career, the happier you will be.

HAVE LOVE, POSITIVITY, AND GRATITUDE IN YOUR LIFE

You have probably heard that the relationships in your life are one of the strongest predictors of happiness and emotional well-being. In *The Good Life*,[17] Drs. Robert Waldinger and Marc Schulz share the results of the Harvard Study of Adult Development, a longitudinal study that has been ongoing since 1938, examining what makes people thrive. Regardless of health, wealth, race, education, and, yes, even career, the number one predictor of wellness was the connection and strength of your loving relationships: family, friends. Spend, make, and savor the time with the people you love. This piece of advice is straightforward but not always easy when you get busy with your career.

When you think about the people in your life, both those who are close to you and those who affect your life on a regular basis, evaluate how they affect your emotional well-being. Jay Shetty, author of *Think Like a Monk*, suggests that there are three types of people to avoid in your life:

1. Those who compare

2. Those who criticize others

3. Those who complain

All three can be unproductive and time-wasting (at best) and will often fan the flames of cynicism and decrease your well-being through their negative energy. It is best to limit your time with people who find comparing, complaining, and criticizing as the basis for their conversations. Again, this seems like simple advice but is sometimes harder to do when you need to limit time with those who are in your life most often. In this case, just do not engage. Don't add on or reinforce complaining, criticizing, and comparing. Eventually, your lack of engagement will redirect the conversation.

When situations are out of your control, an occasional venting session among supportive coworkers and friends can be a reasonable coping mechanism, especially if the conversation helps you make sense of an ambiguous situation, helps you navigate solutions, or helps you manage through a difficult challenge. Support for the challenges in one's life is not the same as habitually negative people, who are toxic. Over time, continually engaging in comparison, criticizing, and complaining will lead to a contagious and unfortunate cynicism.

Cynicism is problematic because it spreads negativity outside of the work situation. *Work-related cynicism* is *persistent* and *generalized* and includes feelings of frustration, distrust, negativity, and pessimism about many elements of your work situation (e.g., organization, leadership, coworkers, clients, the job itself). Cynicism, emotional exhaustion, and reduced professional efficacy are indicators of burnout. Burnout is an extreme form of work-related stress negatively affecting your physical, emotional, and mental well-being. The antidote for burnout, in most cases, is completely changing the work situation, occupation, and so on.

In addition to spending limited (or no) time with negative people, try these to reduce cynicism before it becomes more serious:

- Remember that the grass is not always greener. Leaving a company when you become frustrated with your boss or organization means you are running away from a situation and not toward the fulfilling career you want and deserve. Stay in control and make your changes purposefully.

- Find greater meaning in the work you do. If you work for an organization, many companies are organizing opportunities for time- and effort-based volunteerism. Join in. This will help you connect your company and yourself with the activity of working for a greater good. If you work for yourself or if your company does not offer volunteer opportunities, independently find a volunteer situation where you can lend your professional skills or talents for a greater good. Don't forget that you will also benefit from the helper's high.

- If you are working at an organization, try to gain some control over your workload. It is helpful to say "no" when appropriate and be more assertive if you feel as though you are being treated unfairly in terms of work allocation. If you are performing well, you tend to be rewarded with more work. If you are performing well, you are already valued, so suggesting ways for a more equitable distribution of tasks will not reflect negatively on your contribution or effort. You are setting boundaries and gaining control of your situation, which is viewed positively by most people.

- Spend more time with colleagues and friends who are positive and supportive, while avoiding coworkers who are chronic complainers, criticizers, or comparers. If one of your coworkers comes to you and asks, "Would you like to join me at lunch and listen to me complain about our jobs, our bosses, and our coworkers? I'm buying!" just thank them for the offer and politely decline. You might be surprised to learn how profoundly the energy level of your coworkers will influence your own mood and energy level.

- Try to see "good" in your surly supervisor, mismanaged company, distant coworkers, clients, and so on. Some people are wired to be more negative and pessimistic. If you have this tendency, try to consciously shape your own behaviors by forcing yourself to observe the positives. It might seem contrived, but, over time, it might help shape your cynical attitudes.

- Leave. If your work situation is truly toxic and you are moving toward something that is career- and life-enhancing, we suggest you begin looking for a new job while you are currently in one. The Great Resignation gave us evidence of this as a strategy. If a bad work situation is not likely to change, protect your physical and emotional well-being and find a new opportunity.

Numerous controlled experiments have shown that those who engage in activities to identify the things for which they are grateful have higher levels of well-being. These activities might be writing down the things for which you are grateful in a gratitude journal every day, meditating on the good things in your life, or thanking God for blessings if you are religious. A daily dose of gratitude can be shown for those things in your past or the things that happened throughout the day. You can be grateful for circumstances, outcomes, or relationships—really anything that matters to you. Paula uses reminder cues, such as finding a penny on the street or seeing a time on a clock to stop for a few seconds and recall something or someone for which she is grateful. Another nice prompt is to never miss an opportunity to say "thank you" when interacting with others.

Anyone who has ever made a New Year's resolution knows that, although well-intentioned on January first, the motivation for changing a bad habit or adding a good habit dissolves by mid-February. We are human, creatures of habit, and not likely to change. Change for us needs to be more purposeful, behavioral, and connected to a greater lifestyle goal, such as your fulfilling career acts.

Think through the changes you would like to make for the sake of improving your career. This might be the bad habits you would like to shed and the good habits you would like to add. Be specific. Make them behavioral. Start small. For example, rather than saying "I'd like to volunteer," commit to something specific, such as: "Once a week I will volunteer to walk the dogs at the animal shelter for one hour." Or, instead of "I'd like to eat better," do something specific like have a piece of fruit for your midday snack. Instead of "I will exercise," commit to walking at lunchtime three days each week. The small and manageable changes are steps toward a greater goal, improved physical and emotional health.

As we've discussed in this chapter, building a fulfilling career requires increased physical stamina and emotional strength. This chapter provides many suggestions for behaviors we hope you'll consider changing today to make your career and life thrive tomorrow.

KEY TAKEAWAYS

- Building your career requires energy. Increasing your mental and physical well-being will help you marshal more resources to pursue more.

- Eat well. Didn't your parents and caregivers tell you that "you are what you eat"? Try to eat food you can pronounce, spell, and even draw.

- Get enough high-quality sleep. Getting sleep is more important than toiling longer hours with less productively.

- Laugh and exercise. *Bonus if you can do them at the same time.* Both will improve your well-being long after you leave the gym or the comedy club.

- Volunteer. Lending your time and talents to a cause you believe in will give you energy and an emotional lift.

- Engage in mindfulness and learn to meditate. This is a great way to remain present and centered.

- Take a vacation, staycation, or tech-holiday when needed. Everyone is busy but time away and unplugged is a way to rejuvenate your mind and body.

- Surround yourself with love and people who are positive.

- Be grateful. The act of gratitude changes your frame of reference to be more positive.

SOCIAL MEDIA CHALLENGES

These challenges are a way to showcase the different ways you have protected and leveraged your resources in your career journey. Post these to Instagram, Facebook, LinkedIn, or whatever social media platform you use. When you post, please tag #LiveforaLiving and the hashtag for the challenge.

1. #SkillSwap

Do you have a skill that can be bartered for something you don't do so well? If so, see if you can start a "skill swap" in your network. Swap the tasks you do well (e.g., copy editing, web design, creating a budget) for the ones you don't do well (e.g., cooking, photo editing, creating spreadsheets). Share the results.

2. #BestTimeSavingHack

Create a video or post sharing your favorite time-saving tip or strategy. It could be anything that works for you such as meal prep or the use of a time management technique, such as time blocking. Invite your network to share their best time-saving hack.

3. #DemolishDebt

Share your best tips for paying off debt and saving money. Offer advice on what worked for you. You could share, for example, how to save money on groceries, your favorite budget tip that saved you money, a website where you find great bargains, or your favorite money management app.

4. #ForMyWellBeing

Share your best tips for enhancing your emotional and physical well-being. Offer advice on the strategies and approaches that worked for you. You

continued

could share, for example, your favorite place to walk in nature, a meditation app that you enjoy, or a best workout routine.

5. #MyPriority
Share an image that represents your top priority as you *Live for a Living*. This image should represent *why* you work. It could be an image of the joy you feel in your career, a moment of pride, or an image of your loved ones.

6. #TimeWellSpent
Share a photo or video of the most meaningful aspects of your personal and professional life and, possibly, how these integrate. It could be, for example, an image of you engaging in skill-based volunteering (where you share your professional skills with others) or pursuing a growth opportunity (e.g., taking a class in something).

CONCLUSION

We are grateful that you stayed with us to the end of this book and hope you appreciated the advice along the way. Writing this book was part of our give-back phase because we know that life, while far from perfect, can be a beautiful journey filled with countless opportunities for rich experiences and joy-filled career moments.

The one message we want you to gain from this book is to take personal ownership of your career acts through all the phases of the journey. You have choices to make; time, money, and energy to allocate; and a life to live (and harmonize). No employer, no boss or mentor, no professor or teacher, no parent, partner, or spouse—no one—will be able to create the career journey that is right for you; it is your responsibility to create your own fulfilling career. Love it or dread it—it's yours. We want you to love it—every phase of it.

There are no words on a page that can directly give you an ideal career. It is your turn to put the ideas contained in these pages into action. You deserve the opportunity to have the chance to dream, explore, and prosper. You need to dream to stoke the creative energies that allow you to see what might be possible. You need to explore to uncover how to get there—and learn what you enjoy, how you like to work, what comes naturally, and the path to pursue those that will be most fulfilling for you. You need to take the first step in the career journey so you can *Live for a Living*.

The critical concepts to *Live for a Living*

We all have purchased books with the best intention of finishing them. Then, life just gets in the way. In case you jumped over some chapters, here are some key takeaways, the mindset shift, and behavioral changes we want for you as you direct your career journey:

- **Reframe your relationship with the concept of *work*.** As you advance along your career path, your focus should be on how you direct your *career journey* as it moves you closer to your goals—not your résumé. You decide where you want to take your career, being honest about your talents, your resources, and your priorities. While you might not like your current situation, you are still in control. Shed the belief that there is no way out and any other self-defeating ideas that keep you from creating a career plan. Self-doubt and negativity will always leave you with mediocrity in your career. At the same time, unfounded optimism, in the absence of a career plan, will not result in a fulfilling, ideal career.

- **Explore your career possibilities and allow yourself to have an ideal career.** It is not naïve to give yourself the luxury of envisioning your ideal career. If you are too jaded to dream as an adult, try to remember what your childhood dreams were as there is likely some adult insight that can be gleaned from those childhood dreams. You may not realize your childhood dream of a Nobel Prize in Economics, but a fulfilling career in business may well be within reach. If you are really stuck at the gate and cannot think of anything you would want to do, then ask a close friend, a partner, or anyone who loves you and knows you well. They will have suggestions because they have seen you at moments when you are at your best. These conversations are free—so are your dreams.

- **Stop following the outdated career advice to "pay your dues."** You don't need to dislike what you do *just because* it's work. Work requires commitment and some moments of frustration but should not be a source of dread in your life. If you believe you need to "pay your dues" or "do your time" in a state of dread, then your relationship with work will need to change. The Myth of Sisyphus, the ancient Greek story of the man who was condemned to eternally push a rock up a hill only to see it roll down when he reached the top, was *not* meant to be a metaphor for your job. Do not passively wait for your organization to move you into a career act you want. Remember that keeping you happy is not why organizations are in business. Focus on how you can actively gain the knowledge, skills, and abilities you need from your present job, thinking of it as a career act in the journey. You need to remain in control.

- **With each career act, move closer to your ideal career.** *If your job is not moving you closer to the career you want, why are you staying in it?* Plan your exit. Plan how you will build your next career act. Don't make a wild leap without a safety net, but start building another career act to make your exit from your job less stressful. Always remember when you leave an employer, you should be doing so to move toward a new career act with purpose, rather than running away from something you disliked.

- **Manage your career the way one would manage an investment portfolio.** Everyone has a different tolerance for risk. Just like financial investments, some career acts are considered a high risk, but offer an associated high reward, if successful. Other career acts grow more slowly and are steady sources of income. Think of your overall career as an investment portfolio, possibly mixing higher-risk career acts with some slow and steady career acts. Plan your career journey to be comfortable for your level of risk and stage of life.

- **Use your life priorities and values to guide how you construct your career.** Be certain to have a self-awareness of your life priorities and work-related values. These will set up the parameters within which you can build an ideal career that enhances the life you want. Re-evaluate often as priorities can shift over time, possibly creating a desirable detour in your career journey. Too many people stay with a career path that only fits them during a period of their life. If you stay in control of your career, you will allow yourself to change paths.

- **Protect your resources and remain true to your values.** Your time, money, energy, and well-being are all resources affecting the success of your career journey. Protect, manage, and leverage these precious resources in a way that is consistent with your personal values.

We know that having a satisfying career and developing fulfilling career acts along the way will take some serious, planned, and purposeful effort on your part. We know the ride, as you progress in your career, is not necessarily going to be linear. Opportunities might appear that open a new career journey and your plan for career acts will change. We know the choices you make might not always lead where you had hoped and there will be some false starts along the way. We also know that a fun and fulfilling career is well worth it.

Throughout the book we encouraged you, again and again, to *lock in* on your ideal career goal. Much like the traveler, having a destination gets you out the door to start the journey. We want you to begin moving. However, always remember that the goal is merely setting the direction. Your direction can change as your life unfolds. When you *Live for a Living*, the true *ideal career goal* is the way you engage in and embrace each step along the way. You direct each step. Savor the journey.

Let's stay connected

If certain pieces of advice in this book resonated for you, please let us know and share them with those in your network. We want to hear how

YOU live for a living! Let us know what helped you most with the hashtag **#LiveforaLiving**.

To stay in touch and for more career and life advice, please follow us on Instagram and LinkedIn.

- Paula's Instagram: DrPaulaCaligiuri
- Paula's LinkedIn: www.linkedin.com/in/paulacaligiuri
- Andy's Instagram: AndyPalmr
- Andy's LinkedIn: www.linkedin.com/in/andypalmer

In addition to social media, you are welcome to access the free career assessment tools on www.myJournii.com. On this site, you will be able to create a readiness dashboard, assess your career values, and diagnose your career's safety net with a CURVE assessment.

These tools are available to you and **anyone in your network**. Feel free to share www.myJournii.com.

We want you to feel empowered. Your professional choices hold the power to define your purpose, ignite your passion, and provide you with a sense of life satisfaction. Take control of your career journey and pave the way for your life you most want to live.

This book, we hope, gave you a way to make intentional career choices, pursue meaningful opportunities, and create your best life—a life that is fully and deeply lived.

We wish you great success,
Paula and Andy

NOTES

INTRODUCTION

1.   Fuller, J., & Kerr, W. (2022, March 23). The Great Resignation didn't start with the pandemic. *Harvard Business Review*. https://hbr.org/2022/03/the-great-resignation-didnt-start-with-the-pandemic

2.   Vozza, S. The "Great Resignation" is here. This is how employers should prepare. (2021, June 15). *Fast Company*. https://www.fastcompany.com/90646274/the-great-resignation-is-here-this-is-how-employers-should-prepare

CHAPTER 1

1.   The quotes from Alberto Bravo in this chapter are derived from an interview the authors conducted with him for this book on March 1, 2022.

2.   Fuller, B., & Marler, L. (2009). Change driven by nature: A meta-analytic review of the proactive personality literature. *Journal of Vocational Behavior, 75*(3), 329–345.

3.   Wiernik, B.M., & Kostal, J.W. (2019). Protean and boundaryless career orientations: A critical review and meta-analysis. *Journal of Counseling Psychology, 66*(3), 280–307.

4.   Hall, D.T., Yip, J., & Doiron, K. (2018). Protean careers at work: Self-direction and values orientation in psychological success. *Annual Review of Organizational Psychology and Organizational Behavior, 5*(1), 129–156.

5.   Lievens, F., & Slaughter, J.E. (2016). Employer image and employer branding: What we know and what we need to know. *Annual Review of Organizational Psychology and Organizational Behavior, 3*(1), 407–440.

6.   Younis, R.A.A., & Hammad, R. (2021). Employer image, corporate image, and organizational attractiveness: The moderating role of social identity consciousness. *Personnel Review, 50*(1), 244–263.

7.   Levanon, G., Abel, A.L., Li, A., & Rong, C. (2021). Satisfaction 2021: Job satisfaction remains high even in the midst of the pandemic and economic chaos. *The Conference Board*. https://www.conference-board.org/research/job-satisfaction/job-satisfaction-2021-report

8. Rudolph, C.W., Lavigne, K.N., & Zacher, H. (2017). Career adaptability: A meta-analysis of relationships with measures of adaptivity, adapting responses, and adaptation results. *Journal of Vocational Behavior, 98*, 17–34.

CHAPTER 2

1. The quotes from Omer Trajman in this chapter are derived from an interview the authors conducted with him for this book on November 12, 2021.

2. Harter, J. (2021, updated 2022). U.S. employee engagement data hold steady in first half of 2021. *GALLUP*. https://www.gallup.com/workplace/352949/employee-engagement-holds-steady-first-half-2021.aspx

3. De Smet, A., Dowling, B., Mugayar-Baldocchi, M., & Schaninger, B. (2021). 'Great Attrition' or 'Great Attraction'? The choice is yours. *McKinsey Quarterly*. https://www.mckinsey.com/capabilities/people-and-organizational-performance/our-insights/great-attrition-or-great-attraction-the-choice-is-yours/

4. Tsekova, D. (2021). More than a third of Americans are considering quitting their jobs: poll. *yahoo!*, https://news.yahoo.com/americans-are-considering-quitting-their-jobs-145258951.html

5. Csíkszentmihályi, M. (1990). *Flow: The psychology of optimal experience* (first edition). New York: Harper Collins.

6. Schutte, N.S., & Malouff, J.M. (2023). The connection between mindfulness and flow: A meta-analysis. *Personality and Individual Differences, 200*. https://www.sciencedirect.com/science/article/abs/pii/S0191886922003762

7. Roberts, L., Dutton, J., Spreitzer, G., Heaphy, E., & Quinn, R. (2005, October 1). Composing the reflected best-self portrait: Building pathways for becoming extraordinary in work organizations. *Academy of Management Review, 30*. https://doi.org/10.5465/AMR.2005.18378874

8. Alderfer, C.P. (1972). *Existence, relatedness, and growth: Human needs in organizational settings*. New York: Free Press; McClelland, D.C. (1987). *Human motivation*. Cambridge University Press; Ryan, R.M., & Deci, E.L. (2000). Self-determination theory and the facilitation of intrinsic motivation, social development, and well-being. *American Psychologist, 55*(1), 68–78.

9. Schein, E. (1996). *Career anchors, discovering your real values*. Oxford: Pfeiffer.

10. This career anchor was added by Dr. Vesa Suutari and his colleagues, based on their research studies; Suutari, V., & Taka, M. (2004). Career anchors of managers with global careers. *Journal of Management Development, 23*, 833–847.

CHAPTER 3

1. The quotes from Rana el Kaliouby in this chapter are derived from an interview the authors conducted with her for this book on February 4, 2022.

2. el Kaliouby, R. (2020). *Girl decoded: A scientist's quest to reclaim our humanity by bringing emotional intelligence to technology*. New York: Currency.

3. Cho, Y.J., & Perry, J.L. (2012). Intrinsic motivation and employee attitudes: Role of managerial trustworthiness, goal directedness, and extrinsic reward expectancy. *Review of Public Personnel Administration, 32*(4), 382–406.

4. Akosah-Twumasi, P., Emeto, T.I., Lindsay, D., Tsey, K., & Malau-Aduli, B. (2018). A systematic review of factors that influence youths career choices—The role of culture. *Frontiers in Education, 3.*

5. Roberts, K. (2019). 32 celebrities who dropped out of school. *Harper's Bazaar.* https://www.harpersbazaar.com/celebrity/latest/g18710124/celebrities-who-dropped-out-of-school/

6. https://www.siop.org/Professionals

7. Blystone, D. (2023). The history of Uber. *Investopedia.* https://www.investopedia.com/articles/personal-finance/111015/story-uber.asp

8. How Spanx got started. (2012). *Inc.* https://www.inc.com/sara-blakely/how-sara-blakely-started-spanx.html

9. Wang, C. (2016). Turn your daily frustrations into a billion-dollar business. *CNBC.* https://www.cnbc.com/2016/05/09/turn-your-daily-frustrations-into-a-billion-dollar-business.html

CHAPTER 4

1. The quotes from Frank Moss in this chapter are derived from an interview the authors conducted with him for this book on November 12, 2021.

2. Torpey, E. (2021). Education pays, 2020. *Career Outlook.* U.S. Bureau of Labor Statistics. https://www.bls.gov/careeroutlook/2021/data-on-display/education-pays.htm

3. Silvia, P., & Duval, S. (2002). Self-Awareness, probability of improvement, and the self-serving bias. *Journal of Personality and Social Psychology, 82*(1), 49–61.

4. Lyubomirsky S., King, L., & Diener, E. (2005). The benefits of frequent positive affect: Does happiness lead to success? *Psychological Bulletin, 131*(6), 803–855. https://doi.org/10.1037/0033-2909.131.6.803

5. Kehoe, R.R., Collings, D.G., & Cascio, W.F. (2023). Simply the best? Star performers and high-potential employees: Critical reflections and a path forward for research and practice. *Personnel Psychology, 76,* 585–615. https://doi.org/10.1111/peps.12558

6. Yang, F., & Chau, R. (2016). Proactive personality and career success. *Journal of Managerial Psychology, 31*(2), 467–482.

7. Seibert, S.E., Crant, J.M., & Kraimer, M.L. (1999). Proactive personality and career success. *Journal of Applied Psychology, 84*(3), 416–427.

8. Dweck, C. (2017). *Mindset: Changing the way you think to fulfill your potential.* Little Brown.

9. Han, S.J., & Sticha, V. (2020). Growth mindset for human resource development: A scoping review of the literature with recommended interventions. *Human Resource Development Review, 19*(3), 309–331.

10. Keller, G., & Papasan, J. (2013). *The one thing: The surprisingly simple truth behind extraordinary results.* Bard Press.

11. McKeown, G. (2014). *Essentialism: The disciplined pursuit of less.* Crown Publishing Group.

12. Slemp, G.R., Kern, M.L., Patrick, K.J., & Ryan, R.M. (2018). Leader autonomy support in the workplace: A meta-analytic review. *Motivation and Emotion, 42*(5), 706–724.

13. Weber, B., & Hertel, G. (2007). Motivation gains of inferior group members: A meta-analytical review. *Journal of Personality and Social Psychology, 93*(6), 973–993.

14. Allan, B.A., Batz-Barbarich, C., Sterling, H.M., & Tay, L. (2019). Outcomes of meaningful work: A meta-analysis. *Journal of Management Studies, 56*(3), 500–528.

15. Allen, T.D., Eby, L.T., Poteet, M.L., Lentz, E., & Lima, L. (2004). Career benefits associated with mentoring for protégés: A meta-analysis. *Journal of Applied Psychology, 89*(1), 127–136.

16. La Rue, C.J., Haslam, C., & Steffens, N.K. (2022). A meta-analysis of retirement adjustment predictors. *Journal of Vocational Behavior, 136.* https://doi.org/10.1016/j.jvb.2022.103723

17. Ghosh, R., & Reio, T.G. (2013). Career benefits associated with mentoring for mentors: A meta-analysis. *Journal of Vocational Behavior, 83*(1), 106–116.

18. Chua, R.Y.J., Ingram, P., & Morris, M.W. (2008). From the head and the heart: Locating cognition- and affect-based trust in managers' professional networks. *The Academy of Management Journal, 51*(3), 436–452.

19. Son, S., & Kim, D.-Y. (2013). What makes protégés take mentors' advice in formal mentoring relationships? *Journal of Career Development, 40*(4), 311–328.

20. For more information about the Centre for Effective Altruism, see www.centreforeffectivealtruism.org.

CHAPTER 5

1. Ross, K. (Host). (2020, November 20). Bootstrapping in America: Author Peter Shankman [Audio podcast episode]. In *TastyLive*. https://www.tastylive.com/shows/bootstrapping-in-america/episodes/author-peter-shankman-11-20-2020

2. Shankman, P. The Geek Factory. http://www.geekfactory.com/

3. Campion, E.D., & Csillag, B. (2022). Multiple jobholding motivations and experiences: A typology and latent profile analysis. *Journal of Applied Psychology, 107*(8), 1261–1287. https://doi.org/10.1037/apl0000920

4. Results reported in Pink, D. (2022). *The power of regret: How looking backward moves us forward.* Riverhead Books.

5. Sessions, H., Nahrgang, J.D., Vaulont, M.J., Williams, R., & Bartels, A.L. (2021). Do the hustle! Empowerment from side-hustles and its effects on full-time work performance. *Academy of Management Journal, 64*(1), 235–264. https://doi.org/10.5465/amj.2018.0164

6. Sessions, H., Nahrgang, J.D., Baer, M.D., & Welsh, D.T. (2022). From zero to hero and back to zero: The consequences of status inconsistency between the work roles of multiple jobholders. *Journal of Applied Psychology, 107*(8), 1369–1384. https://doi.org/10.1037/apl0000935

CHAPTER 6

1. The quotes from Michelle Kydd Lee in this chapter are derived from an interview the authors conducted with her for this book on November 18, 2021.

2. For more information about The Flying Wallendas, see www.wallenda.com.

3. Mark Huselid, Dick Beatty, and Brian Becker have written extensively on the way organizations should manage their human resource capital. They have a series of books and articles on this topic, including: (2005, December). "A players" or "A positions"?: The strategic logic of workforce management. *Harvard Business Review.*

4. Seibert, S.E., Wang, G., & Courtright, S.H. (2011). Antecedents and consequences of psychological and team empowerment in organizations: A meta-analytic review. *Journal of Applied Psychology, 96*(5), 981–1003.

5. Hewlett, S.A. (2014). *Executive presence: The missing link between merit and success.* Harper Business.

6. Dagley, G.R., & Gaskin, C.J. (2014). Understanding executive presence: Perspectives of business professionals. *Consulting Psychology Journal, 66*(3), 197–211.

7. Rosen, C.C., Ferris, D.L., Brown, D.J., Chen, Y., & Yan, M. (2014). Perceptions of organizational politics: A need satisfaction paradigm. *Organization Science, 25*(4), 1026–1055.

8. Chang, C., Rosen, C.C., & Levy, P.E. (2009). The relationship between perceptions of organizational politics and employee attitudes, strain, and behavior: A meta-analytic examination. *The Academy of Management Journal, 52*(4), 779–801.

CHAPTER 7

1. The quotes from Andrea Theodorakos in this chapter are derived from an interview the authors conducted with her for this book on March 16, 2022.

2. Arvey, R.D., Harpaz, I., & Liao, H. (2004). Work centrality and post-award work behavior of lottery winners. *The Journal of Psychology, 138*(5), 404–420. https://doi.org/10.3200/JRLP.138.5.404-420

3. Jin, J., & Rounds, J. (2012). Stability and change in work values: A meta-analysis of longitudinal studies. *Journal of Vocational Behavior, 80*(2), 326–339.

4. van Hooff, M.L.M., & van Hooft, E.A.J. (2016). Work-related boredom and depressed mood from a daily perspective: The moderating roles of work centrality and need satisfaction. *Work and Stress, 30*(3), 209–227.

5. Wolfinger, N.H. (2015, July 16). Want to avoid divorce? Wait to get married, but not too long. *Institute for Family Studies*. https://ifstudies.org/blog/want-to-avoid-divorce-wait-to-get-married-but-not-too-long/

6. The American Academy of Matrimonial Lawyers is a nonprofit association of attorneys who are experts in family law. Their publication "Making Marriage Last" is listed on their website at aaml.org/making-marriage-last.

7. Caligiuri, P.M., Hyland, M.A.M., Joshi, A., & Bross, A.S. (1998). Testing a theoretical model for examining the relationship between family adjustment and expatriates' work adjustment. *Journal of Applied Psychology, 83*(4), 598-614. https://doi.org/10.1037/0021-9010.83.4.598

8. Hao, L., Meng, W., Xu, M., & Meng, H. (2022). Work centrality and recovery experiences in dual-earner couples: Test of an actor-partner interdependence model. *Stress and Health*. https://doi.org/10.1002/smi.3137

9. Brown, K.W., & Ryan, R.M. 2003. The benefits of being present: Mindfulness and its role in psychological well-being. *Journal of Personality and Social Psychology, 84*(4), 822–848.

10. Good, D.J., Lyddy, C.J., Glomb, T.M., Bono, J.E., Brown, K.W., Duffy, M.K., Baer, R.A., Brewer, J.A., & Lazar, S.W. (2016). Contemplating mindfulness at work: An integrative review. *Journal of Management, 42*(1), 114–142. https://doi.org/10.1177/0149206315617003

CHAPTER 8

1. The quotes from Elizabeth Lawler and Kevin Gilpin in this chapter are derived from an interview the authors conducted with Elizabeth for this book on July 5, 2023.

2. For the poll results, see www.apa.org/news/press/releases/stress/2022/october-2022-topline-data.pdf.

3. Kompier, M., & Cooper, C. (1999). *Preventing stress, improving productivity: European case studies in the workplace*. London: Routledge.

4. Aronsson, G., Theorell, T., Grape, T., Hammarström, A., Hogstedt, C., Marteinsdottir, I., Skoog, I., Träskman-Bendz, L., & Hall, C. (2017, March 16). A systematic review including meta-analysis of work environment and burnout symptoms. *BMC Public Health, 17*(1), 264. https://doi.org/10.1186/s12889-017-4153-7

5. Cramer-Flood, E. (2022, June 15). US time spent with media 2020: TV's latest plunge, social media's stagnation, and digital video's coming heyday. *Insider Intelligence*. https://www.insiderintelligence.com/content/us-time-spent-with-media-2022

6. Kröll, C., Doebler, P., & Nüesch, S. (2017). Meta-analytic evidence of the effectiveness of stress management at work. *European Journal of Work and Organizational Psychology, 26*(5), 677–693.

7. Shifrin, N.V., & Michel, J.S. (2022). Flexible work arrangements and employee health: A meta-analytic review. *Work and Stress, 36*(1), 60–85.

8. Butler, A., Gasser, M., & Smart, L. (2004). A social-cognitive perspective on using family-friendly benefits. *Journal of Vocational Behavior, 65*(1), 57–70.

9. Strayer, D.L., Castro, S.C., Turrill, J., & Cooper, J.M. (2022). The persistence of distraction: The hidden costs of intermittent multitasking. *Journal of Experimental Psychology: Applied, 28*(2), 262–282.

10. Hembrooke, H., & Gay, G. (2003). The laptop and the lecture: The effects of multitasking in learning environments. *Journal of Computing in Higher Education, 15*(1), 46–64.

11. Rubinstein, J., Meyer, D., & Evans, J. (2001). Executive control of cognitive processes in task switching. *Journal of Experimental Psychology: Human Perception and Performance, 27*(4), 763–797.

12. Bailey, V. (2022, June 8). 200K to 450K nursing shortage expected by 2025 without action. *Revcycle Intelligence.* https://revcycleintelligence.com/news/200k-to-450k-nursing-shortage-expected-by-2025-without-action

CHAPTER 9

1. The quotes from Bill Drayton in this chapter are derived from an interview the authors conducted with him for this book on January 17, 2023.

2. Drayton estimates that 40 percent of the world's population do not have change-making abilities. He notes: "In the US, we've lost four years of life expectancy in one generation in the low-changemaking counties. We've gone from roughly equal per capita output in changemaking vs. non-changemaking counties, there was about 4% to 5% more in the changemaking counties in 2000. By 2020, that had become 71/29. One world taking off, the other not."

3. Guthold, R., Stevens, G.A., Riley, L.M., & Bull, F.C. (2018, Sept. 4). Worldwide trends in insufficient physical activity from 2001 to 2016: A pooled analysis of 358 population-based surveys with 1.9 million participants. *The Lancet.* http://dx.doi.org/10.1016/S2214-109X(18)30357-7

4. IHME, Global Burden of Disease (2019). Cited in: Dattani, S., Rodés-Guirao, L., Ritchie, H. & Roser, M. (2023). Mental illness. *Our World in Data.* https://ourworldindata.org/mental-health

5. Faragher, E., Cass, M., & Cooper, C.L. (2005). The relationship between job satisfaction and health: a meta-analysis. *Occupational Environmental Medicine, 62*, 105, 112.

6. Haar, J. M., Russo, M., Suñe, A., & Ollier-Malaterre, A. (2014). Outcomes of work–life balance on job satisfaction, life satisfaction and mental health: A study across seven cultures. *Journal of Vocational Behavior, 85*(3), 361–373.

7. Gohari, A., Baumann, B., Jen, R., & Ayas, N. (2022). Sleep deficiency: Epidemiology and effects. *Clinics in Chest Medicine, 43*(2), 189–198.

8. The Oura ring is a smart wearable device, about the size of a wedding band, that uses sensors on the inside of the band to track a variety of health metrics.

9. Berk, L., Felten, D., Tan, S., Bittman, B., & Westengard, J. (2001). Modulation of neuroimmune parameters during the eustress of humor associated mirthful laughter. *Alternative Therapies in Health and Medicine, 7*(2), 62–72.

10. Stress relief from laughter? It's no joke. (2021, July 29). *Mayo Clinic*. https://www.mayoclinic.org/healthy-lifestyle/stress-management/in-depth/stress-relief/art-20044456

11. Stierwalt, S. (2020, Feb. 9). Why do we laugh? *Scientific American*. https://www.scientificamerican.com/article/why-do-we-laugh/

12. Yeung. J.W.K., Zhang, Z., & Kim, T.Y. (2017). Volunteering and health benefits in general adults: cumulative effects and forms. *BMC public health, 18*(1), 8.

13. Khasanzyanova, A. (2017). How volunteering helps students to develop soft skills. *International Review of Education, 63*(3), 363–379.

14. For more information, see instituteformindfulleadership.org/research/

15. Cogswell, D. (2007, Jan. 7). Air New Zealand study reveals vacations help productivity. *Travel Weekly*. https://www.travelweekly.com/travel-news/travel-agent-issues/air-new-zealand-study-reveals-vacations-help-productivity

16. deBloom, J., Geurts, S.A E., & Kompier, M.A.J. (2012). Effects of short vacations, vacation activities and experiences on employee health and well-being. *Stress and Health, 28*(4), 305–318.

17. Waldinger, R.J., & Schulz, M. (2023). *The good life: lessons from the world's longest scientific study of happiness*. Simon & Schuster.

ABOUT THE AUTHORS

 **Paula Caligiuri, PhD** is a DMSB Distinguished Professor of International Business and Strategy at the D'Amore-McKim School of Business at Northeastern University where she hosts the podcast "International Business Today." Paula is also the co-founder and CEO of Skiilify, a public benefit corporation dedicated to helping people build soft skills needed for professional success. Named as one of the most prolific authors in international business for her work in the areas of multicultural effectiveness, global careers, and fostering cultural agility, Paula has authored or co-authored several award-winning research articles and books—including, *Build Your Cultural Agility: The Nine Competencies of Successful Global Professionals*, *Cultural Agility: Building a Pipeline of Successful Global Professionals*, and *Get a Life, Not a Job*. She is an instructor for two LinkedIn Learning courses: *Managing Globally* and *Six Skills to Build Cultural Agility*.

Paula has been a frequent expert guest on CNN with a regular segment called "Reclaim Your Career." She holds a BA from Canisius College and an MA and PhD from Pennsylvania State University in Industrial and Organizational Psychology and is a fellow of both the Society for Industrial and Organizational Psychology and the Academy of International Business.

Andy Palmer is chairperson and CEO of Tamr, Inc., which he co-founded with fellow serial entrepreneur and 2014 Turing Award winner Michael Stonebraker (MIT CSAIL). Previously, Andy was co-founder and founding CEO of Vertica Systems, a pioneering big data analytics company (acquired by HP). Vertica is used by many of the world's most advanced companies (including Facebook and Uber) to manage many hundreds of petabytes of data. In 2010 Andy founded Koa Labs, a seed-stage fund focused on first-time entrepreneurs with technical backgrounds from underserved communities. Notable Koa companies include Upstart (NASDAQ: UPST), PillPack (acquired by Amazon), Carta, and Recorded Future. Andy holds a Research Affiliate position at MIT CSAIL. He has served as a founding investor, board member, and advisor to more than 120 start-up companies in technology, healthcare, and the life sciences. He also served as Global Head of Software and Data Engineering at Novartis Institutes for BioMedical Research (NIBR) and as a member of the start-up team and Chief Information and Administrative Officer at Infinity Pharmaceuticals (NASDAQ: INFI). Andy previously held positions at innovative technology companies Bowstreet, pcOrder.com, and Trilogy. He holds a bachelor's degree in English, history, and computer science from Bowdoin College and an MBA from the Tuck School of Business at Dartmouth College.

Made in United States
North Haven, CT
09 February 2024

48580420R00159